THE FIRE OF GOD
PILLARS OF THE FAITH SERIES

BOOK ONE: John G. Lake in Spokane

Compiled and edited by
Brett Wyatt

RILEY CHRISTIAN MEDIA
SPOKANE, WASHINGTON

The Fire of God: Pillars of Faith Book 1, John G. Lake in Spokane

Copyright ©2002 Riley Media Group LLC

First Printing, January 2002

All Rights reserved. No part of this publication may be reproduced or transmitted in any form or by any means, electronic or mechanical, including photocopy, recording, or any information storage and retrieval system, without permission in writing from the publisher.

Cover set up: Mendi Juntunen

Printed in the United States of America

All Scripture is taken from the King James Version

Riley Media Group LLC
Spokane, Washington 99203-0127

ISBN 0-9708898-1-X

This Riley Christian Media edition is a revised republication of the work originally entitled A.F.O.M. and released primarily in the Pacific Northwest beginning in 1990. Some typograghical errors which occured either in the 1990 edition or the original newspaper articles have been tacitly corrected

Dedication

This book is dedicated to my two sons who have always encouraged me and offered support for whatever endeavor I have put my heart to. Of this earth you are the greatest strength I have and I hope that I can be the same for you. I dearly love you and look forward to the adventures we will find ourselves in as we plow God's fields on earth and avail ourselves for whatever adventures He has for us.

Table of Contents

Preface 9

Life Reference Timeline 11

The Healing Rooms
    My First Year in Spokane by John G. Lake 14
    Aided 8130 Ill Persons (January 3, 1916) 19
    Letter from John G. Lake (January 20, 1916) 21
    God's Way of Healing 23
    Letter to John G. Lake (June 10, 1916) 25
    Sermon by John G. Lake: Spokane 1916 30
    All Night With God Meeting The Spokane Press
    (Tuesday Morning, January 2, 1917) 33
    More testimonies 34
    Extracts From the Testimony of Mrs. Annie Norton and Hattie
    Nielson April 22, 1917 36
    Nine Miracles of Healing   Feb. 24, 1918 41
    How I Came To Devote My Life to the Ministry of
    Divine Healing March 3, 1918 48
    St. Patrick and His Power March 17, 1918 55
    Do You Know God's Way of Healing?   March 30, 1918 59
    Testimony, August 18, 1918 65
    The Power of God" October 8, 1918 67
    Sermon printed in the Spokesman Review,
    October 20, 1918 69
    Story of William Bernard, November 2, 1918 79
    General Letter From John G. Lake, February 8, 1919 81

The Healing Stream April 26, 1919...87
The Old Time Religion May 3, 1919......................................92
Tract published by Zion Apostolic Church in Spokane
Christian Baptism and Kingdom Consecration......................94
Does God Use Means in Healing?
  September 14, 1919...114
Buy Home For Church June 24, 1921 Spokesman Review....120
Organize Apostolic Board June 30, 1921.............................121
Revise Church Trial Method. July 1, 1921...........................122

Newspaper ads and illustrations from Lake's time in Spokane....123

The 1924 Healing revival in Spokane
 Special section featuring articles from the Spokane Press
covering the meetings and letter from John G. Lake
dated (July 29, 1924)..139

Personal Glimpses of Dr. Lake and the Spokane church.............187
    Clark Peterson, church member: "I Was There" 189
    Ray Ferguson, husband of Edna Lake,
    Remembering John G. Lake..193
    Alice Fritsch, remembering John G. Lake............................195
    Ione eaton, remembering John G. Lake (August 26, 1990)...197
    L.G. Lake, son of John G. Lake, (November 15, 1989)
    "Memories of a son"..201

Lake and the critics
    Excerpt from Rev. Beatty's sermon: "Healing By Faith
    Can't Be Expected" (Jan. 17,1916).......................................205
    Lake's reply to Rev. F. E. Beatty...207
    Who was Dr. E.J. Bulgin,..211
    Lake's Reply to Bulgin, .(Feb. 28, 1920).............................. 212
    Who was Dr. Windell... 224
    Lake's reply to Dr. Windell, (Sun. April 25, 1920).................225
    J.C. Allborn letter to editor attempting to discredit
    John G. Lake, (July 30, 1924)...228

Lake's reply to J.C. Allborn..230
Our Reply to All Critic and Inquirers June 23, 1918............232
An Address to the People of the Inland Empire....................239

The last years in Spokane
    The Church remembered by those who attended..................246
    Advertisement for Abdul Ben Shinandar............................250
    Abdul Shinandar is John G. Lake...251
    Radio Lectures on KFIO radio in Spokane.........................253
    Obituaries of John G. Lake.. .292

Bibliography and personal study reference.................................302

Preface:

    History has passed over the memory of the life and ministry of John G. Lake without much detail being recorded. While some books have been written, there is even more to the story.

    This book makes a detailed search of media dedicated to John G. Lake. The reader will find photographs and newspaper advertisements, and important new research including interviews with Lake's parishioners never before published with permission.

    Lake encouraged people to press into the Spirit and to walk close to the Lord. With God's help he brought many troubled homes back together. His ministry went well beyond the tales of great healing we have heard of. He would build up your faith to believe in what God could do and what God would do.

    From the time of his arrival in Spokane, after a miraculous moving of God in Africa the ministry of John G. Lake only seemed to increase. With over 100,000 healings in 5 years, one could not help but be amazed at all that God was doing. The eyes of the blind were opened and the lame were healed. These gifts that were *practiced by the apostles did not pass away with them but remain today for those with the faith to believe. This book offers the story of just such a man of faith.*

Many of the sermons found in this book were placed in the Spokane paper by John G. Lake during the times of influenza epidemics in the late teens. More than once there was a quarantine in place and these sermons allowed the word of God to reach those who couldn't reach the church. Enjoy reading this account of the ministry of John G. Lake in Spokane.

Brett Wyatt
Spokane, WA
January 2002

John G. Lake in Spokane

Life Reference Timeline:

Born March 18, 1870 in St. Mary's Ontario, Canada

Age 16	1886-	About the age of 16, had salvation experience and moved to Sault Sainte. Marie, Michigan.
	1889-	Newberry, Michigan Theology training
Age 21	1891-	Ordination as a Methodist Minister Instead of taking a church, he started a newspaper, entitled "The Harvey Citizen"
Age 23	1893-	Married Jennie Stevens Had seven children - Alexander, Horace, Otto, Edna, Irene, John, and Ted
Age 29	1898-	Jennie Lake healed by God under ministry of John Alexander Dowie
	1900-	On August 2nd wife was accidently shot by four old, thru back, near kidney, Subsequently healed
Age 31	1901-	Moved to Zion City
	1904-	Moved to Chicago, bought seat on Chicago Board of Trade
Age 37	1907-	Baptized in the Holy Spirit
	1908-	Left on boat for Africa
	1908-	On May 15, arrived at Capetown, needed $125.00 to gain entry into the country. John and his family had only a few dollars. Had faith to believe, and while in customs, a man came and gave him $200.00
	1908-	1913 Remained in Africa, preaching, healing, establishing hundreds of churches. First wife dies in 1908.

Fire of God

Age 40	early	1910 Fever plague in the Zultspandberg District. Saw thousands healed.
	late	1910 Boers and Botha adopt Lake's constitution for all South Africa.
Age 43	1913-	Returned to America with seven children.
	1913-	Married Florence Switzer Had five children Livingstone Grier Lake, Roderick, Gertrude, Elizabeth and Esther
	1914-	Started healing rooms in Spokane, Washington, Rookery Bldg.
	1915-	Founded Apostolic Church - records show 200 people prayed for daily.
	1918-	March 23rd 3rd annual Banquet of Praise - talked about his last three years In Spokane and the healing corps.
Age 49	1919-	100,000 confirmed healings through five years of ministry.
	late	1920 Moved to Portland, founded Apostolic Church.
	1924	July and August - Spokane healing revival meetings.. Front page news for a month in the "Spokane Press".
	late	1931 Moved back to Spokane
Age 63	1933-	Bought wood frame Tabernacle on Lincoln and Sharp Streets in Spokane
Age 65	1935-	Died, while still pastoring church at Lincoln and Sharp in Spokane

The Healing Rooms

MY FIRST YEAR IN SPOKANE

The first door God opened here, strangely, was a door in what is known as the Church of Truth, a new thought body. Their pastor was formerly a universal preacher. He had seen Christ through Christian Science teaching. He was a hungry soul. He invited me to preach at his church. I said to him, "my message is not yours. I preach the Christ and Him crucified." He replied, "Brother, preach your message, and as much of it as you want to. You are in the hands of the Spirit of God."

After the first sermon, he invited me to take one of the healing rooms in their church, and pray for the sick throughout the week. God gave wonderful healings. The church was mightily moved. It was a new manifestation of the power of God to them. I was invited to teach their week-day classes on the subject of the "Baptism in the Holy Ghost," God showed me four persons in the church at that time who would receive the Baptism. We continued to minister there for about six months, then started our own work About February 1, 1915.

The first person from the Church of Truth to receive the Baptism in the Spirit was a lady. She received the Baptism at the first service we conducted in our own hall. At the close of the Sunday morning service the Spirit fell on her, and she was baptized in the presence of the congregation. She told me that five years before, while in great agony of soul, she fell on her knees and cried out for deliverance and light and help, saying "Oh God is there no one anywhere who can bring me the light my soul needs and show me God as my spirit craves?" And the Spirit spoke to her and said, "Yes, in Johannesburg, S. Africa." On the day of her baptism and she was under the power of the Spirit, the Lord reminded her that He had fulfilled His promise to her, and that I had come from Johannesburg, S. Africa in response to her soul's call and the soul call from others who needed God.

John G. Lake in Spokane

Another lady was likewise Baptized in the Spirit. They have been beautiful souls, as also the other two have been.

In connection with our work we maintain the healing rooms, open from 10 A.M. to 4 P.M. every day, where the sick and the otherwise needy come for prayer. We also have a hall connected with the healing rooms, where we have our weekday and weeknight meetings. Our Sunday services are held in the Masonic Temple. Sunday school in the morning, preaching at 11 A.M. and the large public service at 3 P.M.

Our work has been characterized with wonderful healings, and many of them.

When I wrote the stories of the wonders God was performing in Africa, to America the people largely said, "We do not believe it." Satan tried in many ways to make the world believe it was not fact. But our work has been under the eye of such competent witnesses of such high character, and so many of them, that Satan no longer can deny the stories of what God has done. The news has reached all the Pacific coast states. People are coming, not the sick only, but teachers, particularly among the Truth people of the coast country, to inquire what it is, and what is the difference, and what do we mean when we talk about the Baptism of the Holy Ghost, and how do you get it?

During the year 1915, 8030 persons were healed. Mr. Westwood ministers with me in the work, and has the adjoining healing room. Mr. S. P. Fogwell, formerly a deacon of Zion City is also with me. He makes calls from home throughout the city with the Ford car. Usually we minister to one hundred persons per day, sometimes more, sometimes less.

Among the cases of healing are three of recent occurrence, which I want to give you. They are out of the usual order of healings, and in my judgement belong to the class of miracles of creative order.

Fire of God

One is Mrs. Pn., a trained nurse, a graduate of Trinity Hospital, Milwaukee. She was operated upon the generative organs were removed, womb and ovaries in July last. In November she was operated on again for gall stones. After the operation the bile broke loose and flowed from her body in quarts to such an extent that death became imminent. Indeed, during the time she was being prayed for she was passed into a state of coma, apparent death, and for about half an hour there was no evidence of life, and no breath passed her lips. Mr. Westwood was with her. He had been all night. It was about 4 A.M. The Spirit of God took gradual control of her being in such power that she was healed entirely of the gall stone difficulty. Her generative organs regrew, and last month she became a perfectly normal woman. She is now the matron of our divine healing home.

The second case is that of Miss K., a victim of glandular tuberculosis. She was operated on 26 times, and was treated by 56 different physicians, and finally left to die. One after another abandoned the case. In one of her operations an incision was made in the lower abdomen. This was done in an endeavor to remove a great quantity of pus that had formed in the body. On account of the tubercular state of the flesh the wounds could not heal nor hold stitches. Three times she was opened up and sewed up, but without avail. The consequence was that a normal movement of the bowels could not take place. This condition lasted for six and one half years. While down in the city she fainted on the street. They were about to take her to St. Luke's Hospital for an operation when she became conscious, and she refused to go. She came to our home and spent the night with us. We prayed for her. On the next day, Sunday, as she sat in the tabernacle in the afternoon service while public prayer was being offered, she said it seemed to her as if a hand was placed inside of her abdomen, and another hand on her head. The voice of the Spirit spoke

John G. Lake in Spokane

within her soul and said, "You are healed." She arose from her chair, and became perfectly normal.

Number three. Mrs. L, the wife of a main street merchant here, fell downstairs some ten or twelve years ago, which caused a prolapsus of the stomach, bowels, and female organs. She became an invalid. After suffering several years of operations and suffering she was attacked with rheumatics and became a helpless cripple. When the doctors had failed, she was recommended to take bath treatments at Soap Lake, one of the hot lakes in Washington, where the water is very hot and very much mineralized. The treatment had this strange effect, that the disease left her body and centered entirely in the right leg. A formation of bone, as large as a large orange came on the inside of the right leg and the bone of the leg began to grow until the leg was three inches longer than the other one, and the foot became almost an inch longer than the other one. Her lungs had fallen in through tuberculosis. She was prayed for one day in the healing rooms, and as soon as she went out to get into her car she was amazed to discover that her lungs were raising up, and her chest was filling out. She was perfectly and instantly healed of that.

Later while I prayed for her concerning the lump on her leg, the Spirit came upon her powerfully and she burst into a great perspiration, which ran down her person into her shoes. The leg which was 3" longer than the other one at the time, shortened at the rate of an inch a week and in three weeks were perfectly natural and the same length, and now she wears the same size shoes on both feet and her legs are of equal length.

Fire of God

Our work has extended into the country round about. We now have a congregation in Bovill, Idaho, another in Moscow, Idaho, the seat of the State University, and another at Pullman, Wash. where the Washington agricultural schools are located. We have another congregation in the north part of Spokane, aside from the central work.

John G. Lake

(The date for this article was illegible on the original document)

John G. Lake in Spokane

The Spokesman-Review
January 3, 1916

AIDED 8130 ILL PERSONS

The Rev. J.G. Lake Claims Greater Record Than Hospitals

"During the year just closed we have ministered to 8130 persons in our healing rooms and in the homes of the people, which is 662 in excess of the number reported cared for by the three hospitals of the city," said the Rev. John G. Lake, overseer of the International Apostolic Congress, in his sermon yesterday afternoon. "Many of these healed had been turned away from the hospitals to die as medically hopeless."

"In the relief of poverty, not through doling out pennies to the starving, but through bringing to them health, we have accomplished more in dollars and cents than the Social Service Bureau did in 1914 according to its report of aid given in that year."

"For several months we have received members at the rate of one a day, and had at the end of the year just closed 16 ordained ministers of the church."

The Rev. Mr. Lake has spent the last week conducting services at Bovill, Idaho, where he preached in the Presbyterian church and reports the members and officers of the church are beginning to practice this ministry of healing.

Fire of God

The Church at Spokane

JOHN G. LAKE, Overseer

Where it is not Fashionable to be Dead, but Alive in God, in Body and Soul and Spirit

Healing Rooms 340 Rookery Bldg
Telephone Main 1463

Sunday Services Masonic Temple
11 A. M. — 3 P. M.

John G. Lake in Spokane

INTERNATIONAL APOSTOLIC CONGRESS
REV. JOHN G. LAKE, OVERSEER
HEADQUARTERS
AND
DIVINE HEALING ROOMS
FIFTH FLOOR ZIEGLER BLOCK
COR. HOWARD AND RIVERSIDE

SPOKANE, WASH., U.S.A. *Jan. 20, 1916*

Beloved in Christ Jesus

Grace, mercy and peace be unto you through Jesus Christ our Lord. By the time this letter is in your hands, our Church will have completed its first year of life and service. The message of Christ as a present day Saviour, Healer and Keeper has steadily gone forth in the power of God. Thousands have responded to the call of the Spirit and realized Him as Saviour and Healer still. The marvelous record that God has written in the lives of thousands of healed--many of whom were hopeless and dying and abandoned by man, cannot be given in this brief letter. The lame, the deaf, the blind, sin stricken and disease smitten of every kind, from many parts of the world, have found in Christ the cleansing power of healing virtue, and have been made whole. What was looked upon a year ago by the unspiritual as religious heresy has become a Divine reality. The statement so widely proclaimed, that the days of miracles are past, has been proven to be a falsehood beyond compare, more persons have been ministered to and healed in our work this year than in all three of the great hospitals of the city.

Fire of God

The Christian world, which has been robbed of the healing power of God for so many centuries, through faithlessness of Christian teachers, now finds the Christ their all in all, the Saviour of spirit, soul and BODY.

We have a strong force of blessed men and women, called of God as ministers and teachers of this blessed truth, who will soon be prepared to enter the field in the broad proclamation and demonstration of this blessed gospel. In their behalf we solicit your prayer and co-operation.

All our work for God and mankind is supported by free-will offerings. We make no charge for any service; we minister to rich and poor alike in Jesus name. We feel that there has been a great lack of consecration on the part of many of those who have been blessed through our ministry, who have forgotten that the sacrifice of others was the means of bringing blessing and healing to themselves or their friends. In order that this work may continue, we earnestly ask that you lay this condition of faith and prayer before God, and respond to this call as the Spirit of God directs.

Your Brother in Christ

John G. Lake

MAKE ALL ORDERS PAYABLE TO JOHN G. LAKE, OVERSEER, FIFTH FLOOR ZIEGLER BLOCK, SPOKANE

John G. Lake in Spokane

God's Way of Healing

By Rev. John G. Lake

God's way of healing is a person, not a thing.
    Jesus said. "I am the way, the truth, and the life..." and He has ever been revealed to His people in all the ages by the Covenant Name, Jehovah Rophi, or, "I am the Lord that healeth thee," (John 14:6 and Exodus 15:26)

The Lord Jesus Christ is still the healer.
    He can not change, for "He is the same yesterday, today, and forever," and He is still with us, for He said, "Lo, I am with you always, even unto the end of the world." (Hebrews 13:8 and Matthew 28:20) Because He is unchangeable, and because He is present, in Spirit, just as when in the flesh. He is the healer of His people.

Divine Healing rests on Christ's Atonement.
    It was prophesied of Him, "Surely He hath borne our griefs, (Hebrew, sicknesses) and carried our sorrows, and with His stripes we are healed," and it is expressly declared that this was fulfilled in His ministry of Healing, which still continues. (Isaiah 53:4-5, Matt 8:17)

Diseases can never be God's will.
    It is the Devil's work consequent on sin, and it is impossible for the work of the Devil ever to be the will of God. Christ came to destroy the works of the Devil and when He was on earth He, "healed every sickness and every disease," and all these diseases are expressly declared to have been the

Fire of God

"oppression of the Devil." (1 John 3:8, Matt. 4:23 and Acts 10:38)

The gifts of Healing are permanent.
    It is expressly declared that the "gifts and callings of God are without repentance," and the Gifts of Healing are amongst the nine Gifts of the Spirit to the Church. (Romans 11:29 and 1 Cor. 12:8-11)

There are four modes of Divine Healing
    The first is the direct prayer of faith: the second, intercessory prayer of two or more: the third, the anointing of the elders with the prayer of faith: and fourth, the laying on of hands by those who believe, and whom God has prepared and called to that ministry. (Matthew 8:5-13, Matthew 18:19, James 5:14-15, Mark 16:18)

Multitudes have been healed through faith in Jesus.
    The writer knows of thousands of cases and has personally laid hands on scores of thousands of persons. Full information can be obtained at the meetings and Healing Rooms, 340 Rookery Bldg., Spokane, Wash. Also at the Masonic Temple meetings each Lord's day at 11 A.M. and 3 P.M. and in many pamphlets which give the experience, in their own words, of many who have been healed in this and other countries.

"Faith cometh by hearing, and hearing by the Word of God." You are heartily invited to attend and hear for yourself.

John G. Lake in Spokane

Letter To *JOHN G. LAKE*

June 10, 1916

Dear Brother Lake:

To the glory of God I hereby certify that the following testimony is a true statement:

After suffering tortures for many years and undergoing three operations my condition had become critical; and I was on the verge of another operation when I turned to the Lord for help and was miraculously healed, and am now a healthy woman. Praise His Holy Name!

Since I was eleven years of age I had suffered with rheumatism, and of late years had been bedridden many times. My suffering had been intense, and those in attendance have had to fight for my life, as it would attack my heart.

About eighteen years ago I had a severe attack of bronchitis, which weakened my bronchial tubes to such an extent that the slightest cold would settle there, causing me weeks of severe coughing, until finally the physicians said that I had consumption and advised a change of climate. I made the change. They told my sister that I would not live two months. The change seemed to benefit me until the last few years, when the old trouble returned with renewed violence, finally developing into bronchial asthma and hemorrhages.

About this time my home was burned to the ground, after which I had a nervous breakdown. I could only speak in a whisper, and scarcely made myself understood then. The doctor again advised a change of climate as my only chance of relief, but this time I grew steadily worse. I would cough all night and until the hot blood would spurt from my mouth, then the bronchial tubes would collapse and I would fight for breath. These spells would sometimes last for hours, not only

Fire of God

exhausting me, but were very trying to my relatives with whom I was staying.

I finally went to the hospital, where I remained for several weeks. Dr. Hein succeeded in checking the cough at that time, also the night sweats, and my nerves became greatly improved. As soon as I became strong enough it was thought best to remove a large fibroid tumor from the uterus. It was necessary to perform an operation know to physicians as hysterectomy. They said I would never menstruate nor have change of life after these organs were removed.

For seven years I had suffered tortures from gall stones, the attacks becoming more frequent and severe and of longer duration until the agonies became so great the doctor had to give me hypodermics of morphia to relieve me, and sometimes after giving me all the morphia he dared he would have to resort to chloroform to stop the dreadful spasms.

Last October, while in charge of the emergency hospital at Potlatch, I had a severe attack that lasted eight days. During most of the time I was under the influence of morphia and the doctor said I could not stand another ordeal like that one, so on November 7, I submitted to another operation for the removal of gall stones. Such an experience! I was on the operating table for four hours. They were working to keep me alive and still remove the gall stones. Then those long, weary days of suffering when I had to lie on my back without moving a particle while the draining tube was in my body through the incision to drain the gallbladder. It is no wonder that my hair turned almost perfectly white.

I did not recover as I should have done: there was some obstruction in the cystic duct which prevented the bile from entering the gall bladder. The opening or the incision through which the tube passed would not close and a fistula formed which drained constantly, keeping me in a weakened condition. Sometimes it would close for a few hours and I would suffer terribly until it would open again.

Many, many times I lay on the operating table during those four long months while the doctor would probe or lacerate that fistula, trying to remove the obstruction or cause it to heal, but to no avail.

I became very jaundiced and my whole system was poisoned with the accumulation of bile. I became very weak and nervous; often becoming hysterical. The jar caused by walking became unendurable. I was losing ground every day.

I finally went to see five of the best physicians in the city of Spokane; they all agreed that there was just one chance by operating again and removing the gall bladder, which some of them said was filled with pus, while others feared that my liver had become cancerous, and there was not time for delay; so the following day was set for the operation, but my sister persuaded me to go to see Rev. Lake. At this time you were out of the city and Brother Westwood received me. I am still thanking God each day for giving me such a counselor and guide. With what patience and tenderness he pointed me to Christ, the Healer. How faithfully he ministered unto me until I became convicted of my sins and became fully consecrated to God. I could never have reached this blessed peace but for his faithful ministry, so that now I can say with David, "Bless the Lord, O! My Soul! And all that is within me, bless His Holy name." Of course, I had my times of trial, and had to pass through the "fire."

I found I had many things to make right between myself and God, but with patience he brought me through until I became fully consecrated.

Eight days before my healing took place the incision healed on the outside and I suffered the most excruciating pains and spasms until upon the seventh day it broke open and the

Fire of God

bile actually boiled out. In just a few hours we used more than a dozen bath towels, besides my clothes, but it drained constantly for about twenty-seven hours and until Brother Westwood came and laid his hands upon me and prayed, and the draining ceased almost instantly, changing from a deep orange color to a bright green. By this time I was in a fearful condition; I was having muscular contractions and nervous chills and my heart only beat at intervals. At one time they could discern no pulse or sign of life for more than forty minutes, but with unswerving faith Brother Westwood kept on praying until the Lord rewarded him with a perfect victory, for when I regained consciousness I was healed. Praise His Holy name.

I had not been able to retain anything on my stomach for many days, but now I could eat anything and inside of two days was a new woman; could run up and down stairs and grew stronger all the time.

All my life I had suffered from chronic constipation but this left, along with bronchial asthma, rheumatism and all my other ailments, and the next week, to my great amazement I menstruated as naturally as when a girl, with no suffering whatever. I could scarcely credit my own senses until the next month the menses again appeared, and I knew that the Lord, through Brother Westwood's ministry, had made me a perfect woman through His wonderful creative and healing power.

The wonderful transformation that has taken place in my soul is the greatest blessing of all. God has been so good in forgiving all my sins and raising up such precious friends and ministers in my behalf that I can only consider the new life He has given me as belonging solely to Him and I want to live henceforth but for His glory.

Since early childhood I had been a member of the Episcopal church, but had always had such a hunger in my soul that was never satisfied until I was baptized by triune

John G. Lake in Spokane

immersion and accepted as a member of your church. Since that time the Lord has wonderfully blessed me and baptized me in the Holy Ghost. Blessed be His precious name. How I wish I had words with which to express my appreciation for the loving kindness and patience with which you and Brother Westwood have always shown me and the marvelous blessings which I have received through your ministry.

My earnest prayer is that this humble testimony may be the means of bringing many more to you to be guided into the way of Truth and Righteousness and hearing the full Gospel of the Living Christ.

>   Mrs. Harriet Petersen
>   W 2017 Pacific Avenue, Spokane, Wash.

HEALED THROUGH A HANDKERCHIEF.

Ruth Anderson, Hultsfred, Sweden, healed of hip disease, was unable to walk for one year. Her sister, Mrs. G. W. Wilson of E2018 11th ave., Spokane, came to the healing rooms with a handkerchief upon which Rev. Lake laid his hands in prayer and faith. It was sent to Miss Anderson, who applied it to her body and the pains and suffering departed, and she is perfectly healed.
MRS. J. W. WILSON.

Sermon by John G. Lake 1916

The wonderful record of the healings of Jesus, and of His other miracles, have always held the mind of man, with a strange fascination.

Until 400 A.D. healing in the church was common. Every authorized elder or minister prayed the prayer of faith that saved the sick. It was only after Christianity attained her great popularity in the fourth century, and was recognized by Constantine as the state religion, that the power of God for healing declined. Since that time the modern church has taught that the days of miracles are past. That miracles of healing, though common to the ministry of Jesus and of the apostles in the early church, were not needed any more, because now the world has become wise, the science of medicine has been developed, etc. In fact, it is usually believed that God does not heal the sick any more, and that the ministry of healing is a thing of the past.

This we emphatically deny. Instead, we proclaim the recognized fact that Jesus is the healer still, and that every man who will come to Him and yield Him his life may receive the healing touch.

There are various methods of healing taught in the Scriptures. First: In Matthew 8:1 we have the story of a leper who came to Jesus and made his own plea for healing, and received on the spot the healing touch of Jesus. There was no intermediary. The man made his own definite request to Jesus, and Jesus instantly responded with His "I will," the answer He ever gave to the sick, and the man was healed.

Second: In Matthew 18:19 we read: "If two of you shall agree on earth as touching anything that they shall ask, it shall be done for them of my Father which is in heaven." This is an agreement of two souls in faith for one object. Many are

John G. Lake in Spokane

thus healed. A husband will pray for his wife, the wife for her husband, the sister for her brother, the brother for his friend, etc.

Third: In James 5:13-15 we have definite instructions concerning what a Christian must do when he is sick: "Is any sick among you? let him call for the elders of the church; and let them pray over him, anointing him with oil in the name of the Lord: And the prayer of faith shall save the sick, and the Lord shall raise him up; and if he have committed sins, they shall be forgiven him."

The Word commands him what to do. He must send for the elders. That is the thing a Christian should do. A man of the world who does not pretend to obey God, can send for whom he likes, or what he likes, but the Christian, the Christ-follower, sends for the elder of the church, who in turn is commanded to pray the prayer of FAITH. And God declares that if he does, He will raise the sick man up. And if the sick man has committed sins, his sins will also be forgiven.

Jesus gave still another method of healing. After his resurrection and just before His ascension, when He was giving His parting message to His disciples, He spoke these remarkable words:

"These signs shall follow them that BELIEVE; In my name shall they cast out devils; they shall speak with new tongues... They shall lay their hands on the sick, and they shall recover," — Mark 16:17-18

This latter method is the one. I feel called of God to use in praying for the sick. As I lay my hands on people in prayer, as Jesus himself did, I believe and expect that God will cause His blessed Holy Spirit to flow through my hands into the one who is sick, and make them whole.

When a minister is ordained to the ministry, the bishop invariably lays his hands on the candidate, praying God to qualify him with the Holy Spirit for the work of the ministry.

Fire of God

In many churches, the bishop or minister likewise lays his hands on the heads of children who are confirmed as members of the church, expecting as he prays that the Spirit of God will be imparted to the child.

The disciples received from heaven the baptism of the Holy Spirit, as we read in the second chapter of Acts. Their whole being was filled with the Spirit of God. So much so that in Acts 19:12 we read that God wrought special miracles by the hands of Paul. So that handkerchiefs and aprons were brought to Him that they MIGHT TOUCH HIS BODY. Then they were carried to the sick, and placed upon them and the sick were healed thereby, and demons were cast out.

The logic of this is that Paul's person was so filled with the Spirit of God that when he took the handkerchiefs or aprons in his hands, the handkerchiefs or aprons likewise became impregnated with the power of God. And when these were laid upon the sick one the power of God that was in them from having been in contact with Paul's person, flowed into the sick one and made him whole.

It was the possession of this vital, conscious, living power of God, through the Holy Spirit, that gave us the remarkable record of the ministry of the apostles in the New Testament. It was the possession of this power that made possible the record of the first four hundred years of Christianity, a marvel of religious history. It is the possession of this same power of the Spirit that will once again revolutionize the church of God, and instead of forms of worship, the mighty power of God will be manifested.

Rev. John G. Lake,
Spokane, Wash., 1916

John G. Lake in Spokane

The Spokesman-Review, Spokane, WA
Tuesday Morning, January 2, 1917

TELL CURES, ALL NIGHT MEETING

Apostolic Society Greets 200 in Healing Room New Years Eve.

TUMOR DIVINELY HEALED

Organ, Removed by Operation, Restored—Tubercular Abscesses Taken Away

According to the Rev. John G. Lake, resident pastor of the International Apostolic congress, 200 persons attended the "all night with God" service held in the healing room of the society, 340 Rookery building. The meeting began at 8 p.m. Sunday and continued until 6 a.m. New Year's morning. Communion of the Lord's supper was given at midnight and at 1 a.m. a lunch was served. There were baptisms of the spirit, followed later by prayer with laying on of hands for the healing of the sick.

"During the service fully 100 people at different times gave testimony of having been healed," said the Rev. Mr. Lake. "Some of the cases were what we call 'miracle cures,' where only spiritual agencies could have brought relief."

Tumor Gone in 24 Hours

"Mrs. Carter, S. 714 Sherman street, reported the removal of a 12- pounds tumor through divine healing. The tumor disappeared in 24 hours. That was two weeks ago and no bad effects have since been felt."

"Mrs Harriet Peterson, former matron of the Palouse and Potlatch general hospitals, reported a cure which we placed in the miracle class. In an operation at the Palouse hospital she had one of her internal organs removed. Five months later she underwent another operation, this time for gall stones. When at death's door her case was called to our attention and we prayed for her recovery. She is now in good health and the organ formerly removed has again been restored."

Cured of Tubercular Abscesses.

"Mrs. Mary Whitemore, North Cedar street, was another woman who gave testimony. She had undergone an operation by a physician in Spokane and tubercular abscesses were found, which had eaten holes in her abdomen. She was dying when we were called, but she soon began to revive. She was entirely healed in her own home and is now enjoying perfect health."

More News and testimonies

F. J. Hauptman, Merchant, Winchester, Idaho.
The following article appeared in the Winchester Journal of August 24th.

F. J. Hauptman of Winchester is a living example of the power of healing other than that of medicine. Three weeks ago he went to Spokane encased in steel braces, suffering with an aggravated case of tuberculosis of the spine. He returned Tuesday evening minus the braces, showing an elasticity of step that accorded youth itself. The Lake system of Divine Healing is responsible for Mr. Hauptman's improved condition.

John G. Lake in Spokane

For the past two years Mr. H. has been a sufferer from tuberculosis of the spine. For a period of six months he was confined to his bed, and for the past five months wore braces in order that he might be able to stand on his feet even for a short time. He had about given up hope of a cure when he was persuaded to try the Lake treatment.

After being in Spokane for six days he discarded his braces and the same day walked a distance of 15 blocks, not experiencing the least fatigue. Since then his recovery has been rapid and he returns home practically a new man.

Mr. Hauptman's recovery may be considered in the light of a miracle. The best medical skills available had failed to bring relief, but by the mere laying on of hands and the expression of faith, in a higher power the ailing man is made strong and an unbounded confidence in the creator made everlasting.

Ruth Anderson, Hulsfred, Sweden, healed of hip disease, was unable to walk for one year. Her sister, Mrs. G. W. Wilson of E. 2018 11th Ave. Spokane, came to the healing rooms with a handkerchief upon which Rev. Lake laid his hands in prayer and faith. It was sent to Miss Anderson who applied it to her body and the pains and suffering departed and she is perfectly healed.

Mrs. J. W. Wilson

Fire of God

The Church at Spokane

Rev. John G. Lake, Overseer

If you think that the preachers of Spokane do not know that God heals, read this.

If you think that the doctors of Spokane do not know that God heals, read this.

Extracts From the Printed Testimony of Mrs. Annie E. Norton, Entitled "The Marvel of Christ's Touch."

She gave public testimony at the Masonic Temple, April 22, 1917. Examined and pronounced incurable by 735 physicians. Dr. F. W. O'Neill of the Peyton building had charge of her case. She was examined by the entire Spokane County Medical Association. The entire medical fraternity of Seattle examined her in open clinic. The medical association of Tacoma examined her. The physicians of Portland examined her. The physicians of Olympia examined her.

She was healed by the power of God, in response to "the prayer of faith that saves the sick." She has given public testimony in Spokane, Seattle, Portland, Tacoma, and many other cities.

John G. Lake in Spokane

Her healing was instantaneous. She was poisoned by cutting her hand on a meat saw. A condition resembling gangrene developed. A brown spot an eighth of an inch in diameter would appear on her body and in a very short time would be from an inch to an inch and a half in diameter and from one to three inches deep, according to the thickness of the flesh on the part afflicted.

The flesh of one hand was entirely consumed in a single night. In the morning nothing but the bone and sinews of the hand remained and the forefinger fell off at the second joint.

Her left arm was amputated in the hope of arresting the disease, but to no avail. She suffered in this manner for four and a half years, using narcotics to allay her suffering, until she became a dope fiend and was frequently taken to the police station to be cared for when found under the influence of the drugs.

At the time of her healing she was in the throes of death. Blind, deaf and speechless. As prayer was offered, Jesus appeared to her-standing at the foot of her bed, spoke to her and said:

"When I heal you, tell all men everywhere of my salvation." He touched the tips of her fingers. A stream of life flowed through her body, her pain instantly ceased, her life forces were restored, her eyes opened, she could speak and hear. She arose from her bed, The Spirit of God coursing through her veins like a stream of life.

Mrs. Norton was taken sick January 1, 1912. Her arm was amputated at the Sacred Heart hospital, April 1, 1912. The bone was found to be in a condition like ashes. Dr. Patten tried to grow a culture but without avail

Dr. Stutz, County Physician, offered a thousand dollars to any physician, anywhere, who could diagnose the case and provide a remedy.

Fire of God

On Thursday night, April 26, 1917, Mrs. Norton appeared for examination before the Spokane County Medical Association at the Old National Bank. In the same room where as an invalid she was examined she was formally examined again. The physicians examined her body, took her temperature, and observed the scars where the disease had ravished her body. Dr. O'Neill reviewed the history of the case, and told the physicians how Jesus had appeared to her, and how she was instantly healed. Mrs. Norton told of her healing and the doctors applauded heartily. Dr. O"Neill said that the sores on her body would burn two to three inches deep, that no other case like it has ever been known, and that now she is perfectly well.

Examination and Written Statement.
R. Blake Baldwin, M.D., of the Joshua Green Building, Seattle, Wash., Also examined her and wrote the following:
"I have examined Mrs. Annie E. Norton and find she has nothing visible to show, except the scars where the disease existed."

Respectfully,
R. BLAKE BALDWIN

Dr. Francis O'Neill, Peyton Building, Spokane, Wa.

Mrs. Annie E. Norton, being first duly sworn, deposes and says: That she is a citizen of the City and County of Spokane, State of Washington, over the age of 21 years, and now resides at the Gandy hotel, on West Sprague avenue, in said city. Affiant further states that she has carefully prepared and read the foregoing statements, entitled

John G. Lake in Spokane

"The Marvel of Christ's Touch; testimony of Mrs. Annie E. Norton given by her at Rev. John G. Lake's service at Masonic Temple, April 22, 1917," and does here and now solemnly swear that all statements and facts set forth therein are true.

ANNIE E. NORTON

Subscribed and sworn to before me this 27th day of April, 1917.

W. H. MACFARLAN,

Notary Public in and for the State of Washington, residing at Spokane, Washington

------

My name is Hattie Neilson, of 505 P.O. Box, Morgan Acre Tracts, Hillyard.

I have been a sufferer for 11 years.

I have been treated by different physicians.

My last physician was Dr. John Taylor of Gilbert, Montana, a physician who diagnosed my condition a growing fibroid tumor and advised an immediate operation. I was recommended to Rev. John G. Lake and advised to seek this good man's help. I was received at the Healing Rooms in the Rookery building and ministered to several times. At the end of two weeks the awful tumor had disappeared and my weight had gone down 40 pounds. In 10 days more, I was of normal size and my weight had decreased another 10 pounds, making 50 pounds in all. I am now in perfect health and am praising God, who, in His goodness and mercy to a poor widow, has

Fire of God

saved and healed me. How grateful I am to the dear friends who directed me to Mr. Lakes's Healing Rooms, to dear Mother Meero, who ministered to me there, to Dr. Lake for his generosity and love, and to Jesus Christ, my holy Lord and Healer.

Your sister in Jesus Christ.

John G. Lake in Spokane

The Spokesman-Review, Spokane, WA
Sunday Morning, February 24, 1918

The CHURCH AT SPOKANE
The Living Cross of Christ

NINE MIRACLES OF HEALING

JOHN G. LAKE, our pastor

founder of Lake's Spokane Divine Healing Institute, where Fifty Thousand Healings by the power of God have taken place in three years. The lame, deaf, halt and blind have found Jesus Christ a present day Savior and Healer. Where Tumors, Cancers, Tuberculosis, Appendicitis, Gall-Stones and all the multitude of diseases that curse mankind have vanished by the touch of Jesus, our Lord.

The Church Services
MASONIC TEMPLE, SUNDAYS ONLY
Sunday School, 9:30 a. m.   Church Services, 11 a. m.
Divine Healing, Preaching and Demonstration
Meeting, 3 p. m.

Services at the Healing Rooms, Rookery Bldg., 3rd floor

TUESDAY, 8 P. M., Bible Study, Rev. Joseph Osborne.
WEDNESDAY, 8 p. m., Teaching on Divine Healing, Rev. Chas. J. Westwood

THURSDAY, 2:30 p.m. DIVINE HEALING, Teaching and Testimony Meeting, Rev. J. G. Lake.
FRIDAY, 8 p. m., Spiritual Life Lecture, Rev. John G. Lake.
EVANGELISTIC SERVICE SUNDAY, 8 P. M.

The WORD OF GOD, that neither World, Church, Preacher, doctor or Devil can deny

Teaching on the Subject of
Healing for the Body

1. HEALING BY GOD, THROUGH FAITH AND PRAYER, WAS PRACTICED BY THE PATRIARCHS.
   "Abraham prayed unto God: and God healed Abimelech, and his wife , and his maid-servants; and they bare children."

2. GOD MADE A COVENANT OF HEALING WITH THE CHILDREN OF ISRAEL. A covenant is an indissoluble Agreement that can never be annulled. The laws of South Carolina recognized marriage as a Covenant, not a legal contract. Therefore in that state there was no divorce. A Covenant can not be annulled.

God tested the Nation at the Waters of Marah, and made a COVENANT with them, known as the Covenant of Jehovah Rophi:
      a. "IF THOU WILT DILIGENTLY HEARKEN TO THE VOICE OF THE LORD THY GOD.
      b. AND WILT DO THAT WHICH IS RIGHT IN HIS SIGHT.
      c. AND GIVE EAR TO HIS COMMANDMENTS.
      d. AND KEEP HIS STATUTES.

John G. Lake in Spokane

> I will put none of these diseases upon thee, which I have brought upon the Egyptians: for I AM THE LORD THAT HEALETH THEE."   EXODUS 15:26

3. DAVID REJOICED IN THE KNOWLEDGE OF THIS COVENANT.
> "Bless the Lord, O my soul: and all that is within me, bless his Holy name. Bless the Lord. O my soul, and forget not all His benefits: Who forgiveth all thine iniquities; who HEALETH ALL THY DISEASES." Psalm 103:1-3

4. ISAIAH PROCLAIMED IT.
> "Then the eyes of the blind shall be opened, and the ears of the deaf shall be unstopped. Then shall the lame man leap as an hart, and the tongue of the dumb sing." Isaiah 35:5, 6

5. JESUS MADE HEALING ONE OF THE PLANKS OF HIS PLATFORM.
> a. "The Spirit of the Lord is upon me, because HE HATH ANOINTED ME TO PREACH THE GOSPEL TO THE POOR;
> b. HE HATH SENT ME TO HEAL THE BROKEN-HEARTED,
> c. TO PREACH DELIVERANCE TO THE CAPTIVES,
> d. AND RECOVERING OF SIGHT TO THE BLIND,
> e. TO SET AT LIBERTY THEM THAT ARE BRUISED."
> Luke 4:18

Fire of God

6. JESUS MINISTERED HEALING TO THE SICK
"And Jesus went about all Galilee, teaching in their synagogues, and preaching the gospel of the Kingdom, HEALING ALL MANNER OF SICKNESS AND ALL MANNER OF DISEASE among the people." Mat. 4:23.

7. HEALING IS THE ATONEMENT OF CHRIST., See Mat 8:1-17; especially verse 17.
    a. Healing of the Leper. Mat. 8: 1-4.
    b. Healing of the Centurion's Servant. Mat. 8:5-13.
    c. Healing of Peter's wife's mother. Mat. 8: 14-15.
    d. Healing of the multitude. Mat. 8:16.
    e. His REASON GIVEN for these healings, verse 17—
"That it might be fulfilled which was spoken by Isaiah the Prophet, saying, HIMSELF TOOK OUR INFIRMITIES AND BARE OUR SICKNESSES."

8. JESUS BESTOWED THE POWER TO HEAL UPON HIS TWELVE DISCIPLES.
"Then He called His twelve disciples together, and GAVE THEM POWER AND AUTHORITY OVER ALL DEVILS and to CURE DISEASES And he sent them to preach the Kingdom of God, and to HEAL THE SICK *** and they departed, and went through the towns, preaching the gospel, and HEALING EVERYWHERE." Luke 9: 1-2, 6

9. HE LIKEWISE BESTOWED POWER UPON THE SEVENTY.
"After these things the Lord appointed other seventy also, and sent them two and two before his face into

every city and place, whither he himself would come. ***HEAL THE SICK that are therein, and say unto them, The kingdom of God is come nigh unto you.." Luke 10:1, 9.

10. AFTER JESUS' RESURRECTION HE EXTENDED THE POWER TO ALL WHO BELIEVE.

"He said unto them, Go ye into all the world, and preach the gospel to every creature. He that believeth and is baptized shall be saved; but he that believeth not shall be damned. And THESE SIGNS SHALL FOLLOW THEM THAT BELIEVE; In My name shall they CAST OUT DEVILS; they shall speak with new tongues; They shall take up serpents; and if they drink any deadly thing; it shall not hurt them; they shall LAY HANDS ON THE SICK, AND THEY SHALL RECOVER." Mark 16: 15-18

11. AND LEST HEALING SHOULD BE LOST TO THE CHURCH, HE PERPETUATED IT FOREVER AS ONE OF THE NINE GIFTS OF THE HOLY GHOST.

"To one is given by the Spirit the word of wisdom; to another the word of knowledge by the same Spirit; To another faith by the same Spirit; to another the GIFTS OF HEALING by the same Spirit; To another the WORKING OF MIRACLES; to another prophecy; to another discerning of spirits; to another divers kinds of tongues; to another the interpretation of tongues:" 1 Cor. 12: 8-10

Fire of God

12. THE CHURCH WAS COMMANDED TO PRACTICE IT.

" Is any among you afflicted? Let him pray. Is any merry? Let him sing psalms. Is any sick among you? Let him CALL FOR THE ELDERS OF THE CHURCH; AND LET THEM PRAY OVER HIM, anointing him with oil in the name of the Lord: and the PRAYER OF FAITH SHALL SAVE THE SICK, and the Lord shall raise him up; and if he hath committed sins, they shall be forgiven him. Confess your faults one to another, and pray one for another, that ye may be HEALED. The effectual fervent prayer of a righteous man availeth much." James 5: 13-16

13. THE UNCHANGEABLENESS OF GOD'S ETERNAL PURPOSE IS THEREBY DEMONSTRATED.

"Jesus Christ the same yesterday, and today and forever." Heb. 13:8

"I am the Lord, I change not." Mal. 3:6

14. GOD ALWAYS WAS THE HEALER.

He is the healer still, and will ever remain the Healer. Healing is for YOU. Jesus healed, "all that came to him." He never turned anyone away. He never said, "It is not God's will to heal you." Or that it was better for the individual to remain sick, or that they were being perfected in character through the sickness. He healed them ALL. Thereby demonstrating FOREVER God's unchangeable will concerning sickness.

Have you need of healing? Pray. Pray to God in the name of Jesus Christ to remove the disease. Command it to leave, as you would sin. Assert your divine authority and refuse to have it. Jesus purchased your freedom from sickness as He purchased your freedom from sin.

> "His own self BARE our sins in His own body on the tree, that we being dead to sins, should live unto righteousness: BY WHOSE STRIPES YE WERE HEALED," 1 Peter 2:24

Therefore, mankind has a right to health, as he has a right to deliverance from sin. If you do not have it it's because you are being cheated out of your inheritance. It belongs to you. In the name of Jesus Christ go after it and get it.

If your faith is weak, call for those who believe, and to whom the prayer of faith and the ministry of healing have been committed.

JOHN G. LAKE, Overseer
INTERNATIONAL APOSTOLIC CONGRESS

Fire of God

The Spokesman-Review, Spokane, WA
Sunday Morning, March 3, 1918

HOW I CAME TO DEVOTE MY LIFE TO THE MINISTRY OF HEALING
By REV. JOHN G. LAKE

No one could understand the tremendous hold that the revelation of Jesus as a present day healer took on my life, and what it meant to me, unless they understood my environment.

I was one of sixteen children. Our parents were strong, vigorous, healthy people. My mother died at the age of seventy-five, and my father still lives and is seventy-seven.

Before my knowledge and experience of the Lord as our healer we buried eight members of the family. A strange train of sickness, resulting-in-death, had followed the family, and for thirty-two years some member of the family was an invalid. The home was never without the shadow of sickness during all this long period. When I think back over my boyhood and young manhood there comes to my mind remembrances like a nightmare of sickness, doctors, nurses, hospitals, hearses, funerals, graveyards and tombstones, a sorrowing household, broken hearted mother and grief-stricken father, struggling to forget the sorrows of the past in order to assist the living members of the family, who needed their love and care.

At the time Christ was revealed to us as our healer my brother, who had been an invalid for twenty-two years, and upon whom father had spent a fortune for unavailing medical assistance, was dying. He bled incessantly from his kidneys, and was kept alive through assimilation of blood-creating foods almost as fast as it flowed from his person. I've never known any other man to suffer so extremely and so long as he did.

John G. Lake in Spokane

A sister, thirty-four years of age, was then dying with five cancers in her left breast, having been operated on five times at Harper's Hospital, Detroit, Mich., by Dr. Karstens, a German surgeon of repute, and turned away to die. There was a large core cancer, and after the operations four other heads developed — five in all.

Another sister lay dying of an issue of blood. Gradually day by day her life blood flowed away until she was in the very throes of death.

I had married and established my own home. Very soon after our marriage the same train of conditions that had followed my father's family appeared in mine. My wife became an invalid from heart disease and tuberculosis. She would lose her heart action and lapse into unconsciousness. Sometimes I would find her lying unconscious on the floor, having been suddenly stricken, sometimes in her bed. Stronger and stronger stimulants became necessary in order to revive the action of the heart, until finally we were using nitroglycerine tablets in a final heroic effort to stimulate heart action. After these heart spells she would remain in a semi-paralytic state for weeks, the result of over-stimulation, the physicians said.

But in the midst of the deepest darkness, when baffled physicians stood back and acknowledged their inability to help, when the cloud of darkness and death was again hovering over the family, suddenly the light of God broke through into our soul, through the message of one Godly minister, great enough and true enough to God to proclaim the whole truth of God.

We took our brother who was dying to a Healing Home in Chicago. Prayer was offered for him, with the laying on of hands, and he received an instant healing. He arose from his dying cot and walked four miles, returned to his home and took a partnership in our father's business, a well man.

Fire of God

      Great joy and marvelous hope sprang up in our hearts. A real manifestation of the healing power of God was before us. Quickly we arranged to take our sister with her five cancers to the same healing home, carrying her on a stretcher. She was taken into the healing meeting. Within her soul she said, "Others may be healed because they are good. I have not been a true Christian like others. They may be healed because of their goodness, but I fear healing is not for me." It seemed more than her soul could grasp.

      After listening from her cot to the preaching and teaching of the Word of God on healing through Jesus Christ, hope sprang up in her soul.. She was prayed for and hands laid on her. As the prayer of faith arose to God, the power of God descended upon her, thrilling her being. Her pain instantly vanished. The swelling disappeared gradually. The large core cancer turned black, and in a few days fell out. The smaller ones disappeared. The mutilated breast began to regrow and became a perfect breast again.

      How our hearts thrilled! Words can not tell this story. A new faith sprang up within us. If God could heal our dying brother and our dying sister, and cause cancers to disappear, He could heal anything or anybody.

      Our sister with the issue of blood began to look to God for her healing. Herself and husband were devout Christians, but though they prayed for a time, prayer seemed unanswered, until one night I received a telephone call saying that if I wished to see her in life I must come to her bedside at once. On arriving I found that death was already upon her. She had passed into unconsciousness. The body was cold. No pulsation was discernable. Our parents knelt by her bedside weeping, and her husband knelt at the foot of the bed in sorrow. Her baby lay in his crib.

John G. Lake in Spokane

A great cry to God, such as had never come from my soul before, went up to God. She must not die. She could not die. I would not have it. Had not Christ died for her? Had not God's healing power been manifested for the others, and should she not likewise be healed?

No words of mine could convey to another soul the cry that was in my heart, and the flame of hatred for death and sickness that the Spirit of God stirred within me. The very wrath of God seemed to possess my heart. We called on God, after telephoning and telegraphing believing friends for assistance in prayer. I rebuked the power of death in the name of Jesus Christ. In less than an hour we rejoiced to see the evidence of returning life. She was thoroughly healed and five days later she came to "father's" home and joined the family at a Christmas dinner.

My wife, who had been slowly dying for years, and suffering untold agonies, was the last of the four to receive God's healing touch. But, oh, when God's power came upon her I realized as I never had before the character of consecration God was asking, and that a Christian should give to God. Day by day death silently stole over her, until the final hours had come. A brother minister was present. He went and stood by her bedside, and returning to me with tears in his eyes, said, "Come and walk." And together we strolled out into the moonlight. He said to me: "Brother Lake, be reconciled to the will of God." meaning by that as most all ministers do, "Be reconciled to let your wife die." I thought of my babies. I thought of her whom I loved as my own soul, and a flame burned in my heart. I felt as if God had been insulted by such a suggestion. Yet I had many things to learn.

In the midst of my soul storm I returned to my home, picked my Bible from the mantel piece, threw it on the table. And if ever God caused a man's Bible to open to a message that his soul needed, surely He did then for me. The Book opened at the tenth chapter of Acts, and my eyes fell on the thirty-eighth verse, which read: **"Jesus Christ, anointed by God of the Holy Ghost, who went about doing good, and healing all that were oppressed of the DEVIL; for God was with him."**

Like a flash from the blue these words pierced my heart. **"Oppressed of the devil!"** Then God was not the author of sickness, and the people whom Jesus healed had not been made sick by God! Hastily taking a reference to another portion of the Word, I read again from the words of Jesus in Luke 13: "Ought not this woman***whom **SATAN HATH BOUND,** lo, these eighteen years, be loosed from this bond?" Once again **Jesus attributed sickness to the devil.** What a faith sprang up in my heart, and what a flame of intelligence concerning the Word of God and the ministry of Jesus went over my soul. I saw as never before why Jesus healed the sick. He was doing the will of His Father, and in doing his Father's will was destroying the works of the devil. (Heb 2:14.)

In my soul I said, This work of the devil, "this destruction of my wife's life, in the name of Jesus Christ shall cease, **for Christ died and himself took our infirmities and bear our sickness."**

We decided on 9:30 a. m. as an hour when prayer should be offered for her recovery, and again I telephoned and telegraphed friends to join me in prayer at that hour. At 9:30 I knelt at her dying bed and called on the living God. The power of God came upon her, thrilling her from head to foot. Her paralysis was gone, her heart became normal, her cough ceased, her breathing was regular, her temperature was normal. The power of God was flowing through her person, seemingly like the blood flows through the veins. As I prayed I heard a sound from her lips. Not the sound of weakness as formerly, but now a strong clear voice, and she cried out, "Praise God, I am

John G. Lake in Spokane

healed." With that she caught the bed-clothing, threw them back from her, and in a moment was out on the floor.

What a day! Will I ever forget it, when the power of God thrilled our souls, and the joy of God possessed our hearts at her recovery?

The news spread throughout the city and the state and the nation. The newspapers discussed it. Our home became a center of inquiry. People traveled for great distances to see her and to talk with her. She was flooded with letters of inquiry.

A great new light had dawned in our souls. Our church had diligently taught us that the days of miracles were passed. Believing thus, eight members of the family had been permitted to die. But now, with the light of truth flashing in our hearts, we saw that such teaching was a lie, no doubt invented by the devil and diligently heralded as truth by the church, thus robbing mankind of their rightful inheritance through the blood of Jesus.

Others came to our home. They said: "Since God has healed you, surely He will heal us. Pray for us." We were forced into it. God answered, and many were healed. Many years have passed since then, but no day has gone by in which God has not answered prayer. People have been healed, not by ones and twos, nor by hundreds, or even thousands, but by tens of thousands. For I have devoted my life, day and night, to this ministry.

In due time God called me to South Africa, where I witnessed such a manifestation of the healing power of God as perhaps the world has not seen since the days of the apostles. Christian men were baptized in the Holy Ghost, and went forth in the mighty power of God, proclaiming the name of Jesus, laying their hands on the sick and they were healed. Sinners, witnessing these evidences of the power of God, cried out in

Fire of God

gladness, and gave themselves to the service of God, like as it was in the days of Jesus, there was great joy in that city and that nation.

Finally, God brought me to Spokane, where we have ministered to from two hundred to five hundred sick per week. The city is filled with the praises of God because of the blessed manifestation of God's healing power everywhere. People have come from one to five thousand miles for healing. Some have written letters, others have telegraphed, and some have cabled from half way around the world, for prayer, and God has graciously answered. Ministers and churches throughout the land have seen that, though the church has taught that the days of miracles only belonged to the times of the apostles, the statement was a falsehood, and that the healing power of God is as available to the honest soul today as it was in the days of Christ on the earth, and that the "gifts and callings of God are without repentance," and that Jesus is the Healer still.

John G. Lake in Spokane

The Spokesman-Review, Spokane, WA
Sunday Morning, March 17, 1918

A Lecture on Divine Healing
ST. PATRICK AND HIS POWER
By REV. JOHN G. LAKE

Divine healing, what is it? It is healing by the spirit of God, exercised through the spirit of man. Jesus, the Master Healer, not only healed Himself, but empowered His 12 disciples to perform the same ministry. Later He empowered "seventy others also," making in all 82 men who practiced the ministry of healing during His earth life.

After the resurrection of Jesus, just before His ascension, a great new commission was given to His disciples. He sent them to preach to all men everywhere, commanding them to "preach the gospel to every creature," and declaring concerning those believers who were to become disciples through their ministry that, "These signs shall follow them that believe: In My name shall they (the believer) cast out demons; they shall speak with new tongues; they shall lay hands on the sick, and they shall recover."

A common fallacy in connection with the subject of healing is taught by the churches at large; namely: First, the days of miracles are past; second, no one healed but the 12 apostles. These statements exist because of the lack of knowledge on the general subject of healing as set forth in the Scriptures.

In his first letter to the Corinthians, Paul sets forth in order the various gifts of the Spirit prevalent in the church: First, the word of wisdom; second, the word of knowledge; third, faith; fourth, the gifts of healing; fifth, working of

-55-

Fire of God

miracles; sixth, prophecy; seventh, discerning of spirits; eighth, divers kinds of tongues; ninth, interpretation of tongues.

He commands the church in that, "Ye come behind in no gift." All these various gifts of the Spirit were exercised among them.

James, in instructing Christians concerning their faith in God, said "Is any among you sick? Let him call for the elders of the church; and let them pray over him." Regarding this prayer, he said, "The prayer of faith shall save the sick, and the Lord shall raise him up; and if he have committed sins, they shall be forgiven him." He further declares, "The prayer of a righteous man availeth much in its working."

The writings of the church fathers for 400 years after Christ emphasized the power of healing as known in the churches at that period. Certain sects of Christians from the days of Jesus until the present have practiced the ministry of healing, namely: The Armenians, the Waldenses of Germany, and the Huguenots. In later years, the followers of Dorothy Truedell of Switzerland, the Buchlerites of South Africa, and, in our own day, the Christian and Missionary Alliance, with headquarters, in New York, the Church of God, and the followers of John Alexander Dowie, who maintain a city in the state of Illinois in which no doctor has ever practiced medicine and where no one employs a physician or takes medicine. They trust God wholly and solely for the healing of their body. And the national vital statistics show that their death rate is beneath the average city of the same population in the rest of the country.

Since the establishment of the Spokane Divine Healing Institute in January, 1915, Spokane has become the healthiest city in the United States, according to the national record.

We are frequently asked, "What is Divine Healing:" "Is it Christian Science?" "Is it psychological?" or "Is it spiritual."

John G. Lake in Spokane

We reply: Divine Healing is a portion of the Spirit of God transmitted through the spirit of man. The Spirit of God was imparted by Jesus through laying His hands upon the sick. Again and again in the Word we read, "He laid His hands on them and healed them." Indeed, the Spirit of God so radiated through and from His personality that His clothing became impregnated by it.

The woman who touched the hem of His garment felt in her body that "she was whole of that plague." Jesus discerned that "virtue hath gone out of Me." Having faith to touch His garment she received the power of the Spirit into her person. So mighty was this power of the Spirit in the Apostle Paul that we read in Acts 19 that "From his body were brought unto the sick handkerchiefs or aprons and the diseases departed from them, and the evil spirits went out of them."

Students have long since discovered a new science. This new science is known as pneumatology, the science of the spirit. Pneumatology is a recognition of the laws of the Spirit, a discerning of the modus operandi of the Spirit's working its effects and powers.

Indeed, scientists have undertaken to demonstrate the psychological and physiological effects of the Spirit of God in man under certain spiritual influences and conditions. In the operation of prayer they declare that the cortex cells of the brain expand, and as they expand they receive, and retain the Spirit of God. That through the action of the will, or the desire of the heart, the Spirit is transfused through the whole personality, so that the cells of the brain and the cells of the body and the cells of the blood become supercharged by Divine Spirit. That this absorption and retention of the Spirit of God in the person of man produces a chemical interaction. Sometimes waves of heat sweep over the individual as hands are laid upon them and the

Fire of God

Spirit of God is transmitted to them. Persons will sometimes burst forth in violent perspiration, so great is the chemical interaction taking place within.

The power of prayer is no longer an illustration but a Divine reality.

The Church at Spokane

JOHN G. LAKE
Overseer

Call for Thanksgiving and Prayer

Invites every worshiper of God and every lover of our Lord Jesus Christ to give thanks to God that not one of the many hundreds of influenza patients ministered to by us through prayer only have died.

Let our faith ascend unto God for the entire banishment of this plague.

Healing rooms, 340 Rookery building, open every day and evening from 10 a. m. to 9 p. m.

Phone Main 1463. No charges for any service. Love offerings only received.

John G. Lake in Spokane

The Spokesman-Review, Spokane, WA
Sunday Morning, March 31 1918

DO YOU KNOW GOD'S WAY OF HEALING?
Republished by John G. Lake
Overseer   The Church at Spokane

Let it be supposed that the following words are a conversation between the reader (A) and the writer (B).

A. What does this question mean? Do you really suppose that God has some one special way of healing in these days of which men may know and avail themselves?

B. That is exactly my meaning, and I wish very much that you should know God's Way of Healing, as I have done for many years.

A. What is the way, in your opinion?

B. You should rather ask, WHO is God's Way? For the Way is a Person, not a thing. I will answer your question in His own words. "I am the Way, and the Truth, and the Life: no one cometh unto the Father, but by Me." These words were spoken by our Lord Jesus Christ, the Eternal Son of God, who is both our Saviour and our Healer. (John 14:6)

A. But I always thought that these words only referred to Him as the Way of Salvation. How can you be sure that they refer to Him as the Way of Healing also?

B. Because He can not change. He is "the same yesterday and today, yea and forever." (Hebrews 13:8) He said that He came to earth not only to save us, but to heal us (Luke 4:18), and He did this when in the flesh on earth. Being unchanged, He must be able and willing and desirous to heal now.

A. But is there not this difference, namely, that He is not with us now?

-59-

Fire of God

B. No; for He said, "Lo, I am with you always, even unto the end of the world" and so He is with us now, in Spirit, just as much as when He was here in the flesh.

A. But did He not work these miracles of healing when on earth merely to prove that He was the Son of God?

B. No; there was still a greater purpose than that. He healed the sick who trusted in Him in order to show us that He came to die not only for our sins, but for our sickness, and to deliver us from both.

A. Then, if that is so, the atonement which He made on the Cross must have been for our sicknesses as well as our sins. Can you prove that is a fact from the Scriptures?

B. Yes, I can and the passages are very numerous. I need quote two only. In Isaiah 53:4-5, it is written of Him, "Surely He hath borne our griefs (Hebrew: sicknesses), and carried our sorrows:...and with His stripes we are healed." Then in the Gospel according to Matthew, this passage was quoted and directly applied to the work of bodily healing, in chapter 8, 17th verse, "That it might be fulfilled which was spoken by Isaiah the prophet, saying, Himself took our infirmities, and bare our diseases."

A. But do you not think that sickness is often God's will, and sent for our good, and therefore God may not wish us to be healed?

B. No, that can not possibly be: for disease of every kind are the Devil's work, and his work can never be God's will, since Christ came for the very purpose of destroying "the works of the Devil."
(1 John 3:8.)

A. Do you mean to say that all disease is the work of Satan?

B. Yes, for if there had been no sin (which came through Satan) there never would have been any disease and

John G. Lake in Spokane

Jesus never in one single instance told any person that sickness was God's work or will, but the very contrary.

A. Can you prove from Scripture that all forms of sickness and infirmity are the Devil's work?

B. Yes, that can be done very easily. You will see in Matthew 4:23 and 9:35 that when Jesus was here in the flesh, He healed "all manner of disease and all manner of sickness among the people." Then if you will refer to Acts 10:38 you will see that the Apostle Peter declares that He (Jesus)"went about doing good, and healing all that were oppressed of the Devil." Notice that all whom He healed, not some, were suffering from Satan's evil power.

A. But does disease never come from God?

B. No, it can not come from God, for He is pure, and disease is unclean: and it can not come out of Heaven, for there is no disease there.

A. That is very different from the teachings which I have received all my life from ministers and in the churches. Do you really think that you are right, and that they are all wrong in this matter?

B. It is not a question as between myself and them. The only question is, What does God's Word say? God has said in all ages to His Church, "I am the Lord that healeth thee" (Exodus 15:26), and therefore it would be wicked to say that He is the Defiler of His people. All true Christians must believe the Bible, and it is impossible to believe that good and evil, sickness and health, sin and holiness could have a common origin in God. If the Bible really taught that, it would be impossible to believe our Lord Jesus Christ when He says, "A good tree can not bring forth evil fruit, neither can a corrupt tree bring forth good fruit." (Matthew 7:18.)

Fire of God

A. But even if I agree with all you say, is it not true that the Gifts of Healing were removed from the Church, and are not in it now?

B. No, the "Gifts of Healing" were never withdrawn, and can never be withdrawn, from the true Church of God: for it is written, "gifts and the calling of God are without repentance." (Romans 11:29.) There are nine gifts of God to the Church (enumerated in 1 Corinthians 12:8 to 11), and all these are in the Holy Spirit. Therefore, so long as the Holy Spirit is in the Church, all the gifts must be there also. If they are not exercised, that does not prove that they do not exist, but that the faith to exercise them is lacking in God's servants. The gifts are all perfectly preserved: for the Holy Spirit, not the Church, keeps them safely.

A. What should a Christian then do when overtaken with sickness?

B. A Christian should obey God's command, and at once turn to Him for forgiveness of the sin which may have caused the sickness, and for immediate healing. Healing is obtained from God in one of four ways, namely: First by the direct prayer of faith, without any aid from the officers of the Church, praying as the Centurion did in Matthew 8:13; second, by two faithful disciples praying in perfect agreement in accordance with the Lord's promise in Matthew 18:19; third, by the anointing of the Elders and the prayer of faith, according to the instruction in James 5:14 and 15; and fourth, by the laying on of the hands of them who believe, and whom God calls to that ministry, as the Lord commands in Mark 16:18, and in other places.

A. But are people healed in this way in these days?

B. Yes, in thousands of cases. I have myself laid hands upon many hundreds of thousands of persons, and have seen the Lord's Power manifested in the healing of great numbers,

John G. Lake in Spokane

many of whom are living witnesses in many countries, who have testified publicly before thousands, and who are prepared to testify at any time. This ministry is being exercised by devoted Christians in many parts of America, Europe, Africa and elsewhere.

A. But how shall I obtain the necessary faith to receive healing, which faith I am at present conscious I do not possess?

B. It is written, "Belief cometh of hearing, and hearing by the Word of Christ." (Romans 10:17.)

Our meetings are held for the express purpose of teaching fully the Word of God in this matter, and I very heartily invite you to attend the meetings. All are welcome and there are no charges of any kind made, for all God's gifts are free gifts. Salvation is the first of these, without which you can not be healed through faith in Jesus. All the costs of this work are covered by the free will offerings of the people who attend these meetings, and others whom the Lord leads to help; but the poorest who have nothing to give are as heartily welcome as the richest.

A. Do you see the sick and lay hands upon them:

B. Yes: after we feel satisfied that they are fully resting in the Lord alone for the healing, we see privately, so far as time permits, those who attend; but under no circumstances do we claim the power to heal any; for "power belongeth unto God."

A. Have you any writings upon this subject which can be purchased?

B. Yes: these can be obtained at the Healing Rooms, 340 Rookery building, Spokane. But the best book on Divine Healing is the Bible itself, studied prayerfully and earnestly.

We extend to you a hearty invitation to attend the meetings, which are free to all. Our prayer is that you may be led to find in Jesus Christ our Lord and God, your present

Saviour from sin, your Healer from sickness, your Cleanser from all evil, your Keeper in the way to Heaven, your Friend, and your All for Time and Eternity.

We pray that these words may help many who read, and that our little conversation may bear fruit in leading many readers to look to Jesus only.

> "The Healing of Christ's
> seamless dress
> Is by all beds of pain:
> We touch Him in life's
> throng and press
> And we are whole again."

John G. Lake in Spokane

The Spokesman-Review, Spokane, WA
Sunday Morning, August 18, 1918

The Church At Spokane
REV. JOHN G. LAKE, OVERSEER

    Masonic Temple Services, Sunday only.
    Sunday School 9:30 a. m., where Christ as Savior of Spirit and soul and body is taught.
    11:00 a. m. Preaching Service
    3:00 p. m. Special Service, Subject: "The Religion of Jesus Christ, What Is It?"

    Service at the Healing Rooms in the Rookery Building
    Sunday Evening at 8 p. m. Evangelistic Service.
    Wednesday Evening at 8 p. m. Gospel Lecture, Rev. Charles J. Westwood
    Thursday at 2:30 p. m. Divine Healing Teaching and Ministry, Rev. John G. Lake.
    Friday Evening at 8 p. m. Spiritual life lecture, Rev. John G. Lake.

    The Healing Rooms are open every week day from 10 a. m. to 4 p. m., where an entire staff of Godly Ministers will receive all persons who desire personal ministry or interviews. Cut out this notice and preserve it. These meetings are all permanent fixtures.

Telephone   Main 1463, Motor cars always waiting for hurry calls to your home

Rev. F. J. Osborne, a Methodist minister, stationed at Addy, Wash, pronounced incurable by several physicians of Bright's disease, a patient at the Deaconess hospital, Spokane. Analysis showed 15% albumen. **HEALED UNDER DIVINE HEALING MINISTRY,** AND PREACHED AND TESTIFIED OF HIS HEALING AT THE Masonic Temple, Spokane, eight days after being ministered to. The doctors said: "He will die." The nurse said: "You're a fool to think you can be healed without medicine." Osborne said: "I am going to trust God, and regard this discouragement as the voice of the devil." He received the reward of faith. Preacher said: "God does not perform miracles of healing now." A druggist said: "Drugs are no good to him, but I believe God can heal him." Men from Addy, Wash., who were not Christians, sent words of encouragement and faith, saying: "GO TO IT. If there is a God, you ought to be healed. If Jesus ever healed, He can heal still."

Ten months after he was healed this beautiful son was born to bless his home; a living testimony of his father's health and healing, and today Rev. Osborne has returned to visit his old church and friends at Addy, Wash., where he and Mrs. Osborne are conducting blessed Gospel meetings, and from his healing until now many have been healed of God and delivered from sin under his ministry.

John G. Lake in Spokane

The Spokesman-Review, Spokane, WA
Sunday Morning, October 8, 1918

The Church at Spokane
JOHN G. LAKE, Overseer

Lesson Sermon on Healing
THE POWER OF GOD

has always been a mystery for the unbelieving world and a source of delight and wonder to the real Christian who received it. The Disciples of Jesus thought it would come upon them when the kingdom was restored. Jesus corrected this error, by declaring: "Ye shall receive power after that the Holy Ghost is come upon you, and ye shall be witnesses unto me, in Jerusalem, in Judea and unto the uttermost parts of the earth."

It was to be universal for every believer. It was to qualify them to give competent witness of Him, both in word and deed. This is evidenced in that He declared: "Go ye into all the world and preach the Gospel — These signs shall follow them that believe: In MY name they SHALL CAST OUT DEMONS — THEY SHALL SPEAK with NEW TONGUES — THEY SHALL LAY THEIR HANDS ON THE sick and they shall recover."

The preaching of the Word was to be accompanied by power to BLESS, SAVE and HEAL. Not by the POWER of MAN (psychological), but by the POWER of GOD, SPIRITUAL. "For as the heavens are higher than the earth, so are My ways than your ways, and My thoughts than your thoughts." Not by might (man using man), nor by power, (man using God), but by MY SPIRIT, (God using man)saith the LORD of HOSTS.

Fire of God

Agnes Young daughter of Mr. and Mrs. Wm. Young, at 169 ½ Post St., Spokane, was born at one of the hospitals of the city of Spokane, a beautiful child. She suffered from malnutrition, the doctors said. She weighed six pounds at birth, but no food that could be obtained would nourish the little body. The power to assimilate was lacking.

Gradually the body became smaller, growing thinner and thinner. At nine months the child weighed much less than at birth. The fingers had become as bird claws, the eyes were sunken and deathly. The voice became a whine of suffering.

Death, "the enemy of God," was upon her. Then help came. The prayer of faith was offered; the life of God was imparted to her. She was removed from the hospital to a Christian home, Mrs. Estella Mason became her nurse. She was healed of the Lord, and is now a healthy, happy girl of three and a half years of age, the joy of her parents, the delight of friends and the living testimony of Christ's desire and will to heal.

John G. Lake in Spokane

The Spokesman-Review, Spokane, WA
October 20, 1918

**THE CHURCH AT SPOKANE
JOHN G. LAKE, Overseer**

We invite every reader of The Spokesman-Review to join with us in Divine Service

Announcements during the Spanish influenza period of the quarantine.
Our healing rooms at 340 Rookery Building will be open for personal ministry through prayer and laying on of hands every day of the week from 10 a.m. to 9 p.m. Our phone is Main 1463. We will be glad to minister to you for any need of spirit, soul or body.

Sermon By REV. JOHN G. LAKE

"As He is, so are we in this world." 1 John 4:17

The mind of the world is fixed on the Redeemer. The Old Testament scriptures, looking up to Christ, are particularly prolific in their description of His life, His sorrows, His sufferings, His death, His sacrifice. All these were the qualities of the Redeemer. All these were endured and exercised by the Redeemer in order to obtain a something. That something was REDEMPTION.

What redemption means is best seen by following the chain of Christ's life from the Crucifixion on — not back of the cross, this side of it. If you want to understand the Redeemer, see Him before the cross comes into view. That is, if you want to understand the Redeemer who obtained the redemption. But

Fire of God

if you want to understand the redemption that He obtained, look on this side of Calvary.

The great majority of the Christian world is still weeping at the foot of the cross. The vast majority of Christians are still carrying a little crucifix, representing a dead Christ. The consciousness of man is fixed on the Christ who died, not on the Christ who lives. They are looking back to the Redeemer who was, not the Redeemer who is.

On this side of the cross we see all the marvel of opposites to what we see in the Christ on the other side of the cross. On the other side of the cross we see a man of sorrows and acquainted with sickness, bearing our sicknesses, carrying our sorrows. He had nowhere to lay His head. Poverty was one of His characteristics. Nobody ever stops to think, or rarely so, that He bore His poverty, and what for? Ans. "That through His poverty we might be made rich." He bore our sorrows, what for? That we through His sorrows might be made glad. He bore our sufferings, for what? That we through His stripes might be healed. He gave His life a sacrifice for sins, for what? That we should know no sin. Then having completed the redemption, or purchased the redemption, the redemption becomes manifest on this side of Calvary.

I sometimes wish that I could turn the face of the world the other way. You may observe that I rarely turn the face of mankind to the cross. The world looked to the cross until they passed it. But if they had never passed it redemption would be no more a reality than it was before. Redemption becomes a reality as we obtain the redemption. To obtain the fact that the Redeemer purchased is the purpose of the Christian life. On this side of the cross we see the victory, not the suffering, not the humility and dejection and rejection but the VICTORY.

We see the first glory glimmer of that victory when Jesus, who was crucified as a Redeemer, steps forth as the redeemed. For the Redeemer Himself, the first fruits of them that slept, BECAME the Redeemer of mankind, or the pattern of redemption. He was not the pattern of redemption back there on the other side of the cross. He BECAME the pattern of redemption. Paul puts it in such terse terms. "He BECAME the author of eternal salvation." Not "was manufactured the author of eternal salvation," not "was born," but BECAME the author of eternal salvation. Why? Because, having as the Redeemer entered into the redemption by Himself, "the first fruits of them that slept," the first victor, the first example of victory. He became the manifestor, the demonstrator, the revealer, the embodiment of eternal salvation.

On this side of the cross there is the victory of His resurrection, the marvel of all victories, the victory over death, by which He took death captive. A living man Himself, He came forth the Conqueror of death itself, having put all things under His feet. What an ascent into triumph! What a change in His consciousness! What a distinction between the Redeemer and the redeemed! No longer subject to death, but triumphing over it. No longer subject to humiliation, but now, bless God, becoming the exalted One. For in the ascension we see the exaltation of Jesus, instead of the man of sorrows, acquainted with grief, or sickness. We see the living triumphant, exultant Son of God ascending to the Throne of God, receiving from God, the Father, the superlative gift of gifts, receiving from God, the Father, what Jesus and the Father considered worthy of the suffering and death and sacrifice and redemption of Jesus Christ. A reward so great that Jesus Himself considered it worth all His sufferings, all His buffetings, His earth career, His humiliation, His sacrifice and death. All given to obtain it, the GIFT OF THE HOLY SPIRIT.. (Acts 2:16-18)

On this side of the cross we see the distributing of His new life. Not the life, that was on the other side, but the life that is on this side — the life of triumph, the life of victory, the life of praise, the life of power, the life of glory, exultant, triumphant.

The other night as I lay in bed I was thinking and praying over some of the things that were passing through my mind concerning Jesus. The scriptures of Rev. 1:18 came with force to me, where Jesus, not as a humiliated Saviour, but as a Kingly Conqueror, stands forth with the marvelous declaration that "I am He that liveth, and was dead; and behold, I am alive for evermore, and have the keys of hell and of death."

It seems to me that in all the Word of God there is no such shout of triumph as that. Why, it seems to me as if the very heaven and the earth and all that is in them, ring with that exultant shout of a real Victor. "I have the keys of hell, and of death." The enemies of man, taken captive by the Son of God subject to His dictate. That is the Christ that speaks to my soul. That is the Christ on this side of Calvary. That is the Christ my soul worships.

INVOCATION

God be merciful to us, and bless us, and cause Thy face to shine upon us; that Thy way may be known in the earth, Thy saving health among all nations in the name of Jesus. Amen.

I am going to tell you a strange thing. I am not much interested in the Christ on the other side of Calvary. Not half so much as I am in the Christ on this side of Calvary. Bless God, I love the Redeemer, but I GLORY in His REDEMPTION.

The marvel of Christianity, and the wonder of this scripture that I call your attention to, is that it does not say that "as He WAS" back there, so are we to be in this world. Don't you see, that is where the world fell down, where the Christian life became submerged in a veil of tears and shadows and

John G. Lake in Spokane

darkness and poverty and humiliation and suffering. All of which Christian mankind accepted joyfully, because they believed they were exemplifying Jesus Christ, and thinking they were glorifying Him. They still visioned, not the Christ that IS, but the Christ that WAS. The Christ who bore and endured and suffered and died in order to obtain the privilege of the Christ who is, and to become the Christ who is.

Now if I could radically turn your minds tonight clear around from that vision of the Christ before the cross, to the vision of the Christ who IS this fact would mean that your souls must ascend in consciousness and union with the overcoming Son of God. Not bowed and bound with the humiliated Saviour, but joined in holy glory triumph with the Son of God who obtained the victory and revealed it and distributes its power and glory to the souls of men.

"As He IS," not as He WAS, John said, "so are we in this world." Not in the life to come. The glory is not for the life that is coming, but for the life that is now. The victory is not for the future. It is for the NOW. It is not for the good days bye and bye. It is for the NOW. Not for heaven to come, but heaven on earth NOW.

Sin, sickness, death under His feet. Hell itself taken captive and obedient to His word. Every enemy of mankind throttled, bound, chained by the Son of God. Mankind joined with Him by the Holy Ghost in living triumph. Why if I receive of the spirit of Jesus Christ, of the Christ who IS, I receive of the spirit of victory and power and might and dominion of grace, of love, of power, blessed be God, of all the blessed estate of which Jesus Himself is now the conscious Master. All these He gives to the Christian through imparting to Him the Holy Ghost.

Fire of God

Holy Spirit Message

The Spirit of the Lord says within my soul, that: The universal sound of praise in which angels and men, all creatures in the earth, the sea and the sky, will eventually join, comes because the consciousness of the overcoming Christ has dawned upon them and possessed their soul.

Some of the final song, the song of the ages, that shout of victory, we find in the Fifth of Revelation.

"And I beheld and I heard the voice of many angels round about the throne and the beasts and the elders; and the number of them was ten thousand times ten thousand, and thousands of thousands; Saying with a loud voice, Worthy is the Lamb that was slain to receive power and riches, and wisdom, and strength, and honor, and glory, and blessing. And every creature which is in heaven, and on the earth, and under the earth, and such as are in the sea, and all that are in them, heard I saying, Blessing, and honor, and glory, and power be unto him that sitteth upon the throne, and unto the Lamb for ever and ever. And the four beasts said, Amen. And the four and twenty elders fell down and worshiped him that liveth for ever and ever"

Should I carry your soul tonight into the place of victory in God, I must carry it into the consciousness of Christ's overcoming life. All His healing virtue, His saving grace, His transforming spirit, all the angelic communion, the heavenly foretaste, the consciousness of the estate of the redeemed, the glory triumph of Jesus Christ is in the consciousness born from the resurrection and revealed in the Revelation. "For as He is so are we in his world."

Jesus in His earth life reached forth in the spirit into that life and kingdom and triumph and exhibited in this world, in a measure, that victory and triumph that His soul knew and visioned. But when the cross came He entered actually and

John G. Lake in Spokane

experimentally into the life that His soul formerly visioned and knew through the word of God and the consciousness of God within His heart. And so His ministry in the spirit is a ministry in the ALL POWER, ALL CONSCIOUSNESS, ALL KNOWLEDGE, all grace, all victory, all salvation. Bless God!

I would lift your soul tonight in the spirit of God into that glow and glory of the triumphant life. Do you know that it is only as your mind settles back into the humiliation and suffering and the weakness and the fear and doubting of the dispensation that is past, that you grow weak and sickly and sinful? But as your soul looks forward and possesses in the present the glorious victory that Jesus acquired and exhibits and enjoys, does it rise out of its sorrows, out of its sins, into that glorious triumph of the children of God?

Prayer

God, when earth and sea and sky discover the wonder of the redemption of Jesus, then, dear God, the heart will turn anew with a holy love to the Redeemer, who by His beauteous grace dared to endure it all that we might possess the inheritance.

O God, when we think of the marvel of the souls of the ages breaking into a shout of heavenly glory and praise to Christ, because that on our souls has dawned the wonder of His redemption, when the world will say again, "Worthy is the Lamb that was slain to receive honor and might and glory and power and blessing." O God, when our hearts comprehend the purpose of Jesus, when our souls possess it, when that redemption becomes a fact in our nature, when we have been transformed into the likeness and the image and the stature and the fullness of Jesus Christ, our souls will worship thee as they can not worship thee this moment.

Fire of God

But, Almighty God, we look forward and throw our hearts open for the almightiness of a redemption that comprehends the utter transformation of mankind into the image of Jesus Christ. Bless His name forever. Bless His precious name forever! Amen.

It would not be pleasant to always have to live with babies and imbeciles, or with a lot of half grown-up folks. I want you to sympathize with God. I want you to catch the vision of the ordinary Christian conception. Think of God having to live forever and ever in association with people who were not half big enough to comprehend His purpose, His desires, or His will. That is not God's purpose. Jesus Christ undertook the biggest contract that heaven or earth or sea or sky ever knew. He undertook the redemption of mankind and their transformation by the Spirit of the living God into His own likeness and image and stature and understanding in the grace and power and fullness of His own nature. Jesus Christ is the associate of God, one with Him, and with every son of God. He has purposed that redeemed men, grown up in God, transformed into the very image and likeness and nature and fullness of Jesus Christ, becoming like the Son of God, shall be the associates of God.

What did God create mankind for anyway? Answer: "The chief end of man is to glorify God and enjoy Him forever and a mighty lot more."

God's purpose in the creation of mankind was to develop an association on His own plane. Otherwise God would have been eternally living with babies or imbeciles. He would have been compelled forever to associate with those who were not able to understand or comprehend His nature or character or the marvel of His being or the wonder of His power.

John G. Lake in Spokane

The wonder of the redemption of Jesus Christ is revealed in the matchlessness of God's purpose to transform man into His very nature and image and likeness and fullness. Thereby men as sons of God become, bless God, the associates of Almighty God, on His own plane of life and understanding.

When my soul saw the vision of God Almighty's marvelous purpose, I felt like falling on my face afresh and crying out "Worthy is the Lamb that was slain." For "As He is so are we in this world." All the glory and power that Jesus knows at the Throne of God, all the wonder of His overcoming grace, all the marvel of the greatness of His power, is yours and mine to receive through faith in the Son of God, yours and mine to expect through the faith of the Son of God, yours and mine to possess and enjoy and reveal to the glory of God.

Prayer

God, one day we must graduate out of the kindergarten. God, one day our souls must grow up to the stature of men. God, one day our minds must develop to the comprehension and understanding of grownup souls. God, the world is in kindergarten . The Christian world is drinking milk. God, they have not had the vision, they have not understood the marvel of it all. Oh God, we bless three for the Holy Ghost. We bless thee for the baptism of the Holy Ghost, which has been the Revealer in our souls of the wonder and magnificence of the eternal exalted Christ.

God, we bless thee for the grace of God that hath made possible such a union with the Lord Jesus. That being born again of God we have entered into oneness in the Holy Spirit; oneness with Christ that by His grace, His nature and His power are revealed in us and revealed through us.

And my God, help us to go one further and say, revealed by us to the glory of God, the Father, Amen.

Let us now give ourselves to God in Holy Consecration.

Consecration Prayer

MY GOD AND FATHER
In Jesus Name I come to Thee.
Take me as I am. Make me what
I ought to be in Spirit, in Soul, in Body.
Give me Power to do right, If I have
Wronged any, to repent, to confess, to restore.
No matter what it costs, wash me in the blood
Of Jesus, that I may now become Thy child.
And manifest Thee in a perfect Spirit,
A Holy Mind, a Sickless Body — Amen

REV. JOHN G. LAKE, Spokane, Wash.

John G. Lake in Spokane

Spokane Daily Chronicle, Spokane, WA.
Sunday, November 2, 1918

The Church at Spokane
JOHN G. LAKE, Overseer

ANNOUNCEMENTS
During the quarantine our
HEALING ROOMS
at 340 Rookery Bldg., will be open for personal ministry from 10 a. m. till 9 p. m., including Sundays
THANKSGIVING
Out of almost 600 cases of Spanish Influenza to which we have ministered exclusively not one has died.

Story of WILLIAM BERNARD
Canadian Artilleryman
as Told by John de Witt

    I met William Bernard, or "Billy," as his friends call him, some three years ago. We became warm friends.
    He walked with his head drawn over on the side. One day he told me the reason for it.
    "When I was a child of about three and a half years," said Bernard. "I was dropped by my nurse, and suffered curvature of the spine. It affected my whole life. When other children played their rough games I could not take part, and as I grew up and longed for athletics I was shut out. I went to several of the best doctors in London, but no hope of a cure was given. Then I came to America and interviewed other physicians, but though they did their best I still remain the same."

Fire of God

My sympathies naturally went out to Bernard. One day I suggested that he go with me to Rev. John Lake. He laughed and said: "I have no faith." But I kept urging him, so he consented. I introduced him to Mr. Lake and he immediately said, "I have no faith." I remember how Mr. Lake looked up in his face, threw his head back, and laughingly said: "But I have enough faith for both of us."

Mr. Lake prayed with him, then turned him over to his assistant the Rev. Mr. Westwood, who probably ministered to him maybe six times. Then, one day Bernard said to me: "I have always longed to give my services to my country. I believe I am well and I am going to test it. My curvature is entirely gone and my height has increased one inch. I will go over to the Canadian recruiting office and see if I can get in."

Bernard did so, was passed by two physicians as absolutely perfect.

A few months elapsed and he went up again and was passed by three more physicians.

On account of the stringency of acceptance by Canada, they told him to go to Nelson, B.C., and enlist. He did so, was re-examined there by two physicians and passed for the third time, and today I received a letter from him from England, saying that he was a full-fledged artilleryman, never felt better in his life, expected to go to France shortly, and hoped soon to have the pleasure of walking down Riverside with me again, "as everybody here, inclusive of myself, believes the war will soon be over."

John G. Lake in Spokane

The Spokane Daily Chronicle
Saturday February, 8, 1919

THE CHURCH at SPOKANE
JOHN G. LAKE, Overseer
Headquarters, Offices and Divine Healing Rooms
340 Rookery Building, Cor. Howard and Riverside
Phone, Main 1463

GENERAL LETTER

Beloved Brothers and Sisters in Christ Jesus and all the multitude of friends and well-wishers, to all who rejoice with us in the knowledge of the blessedness of real salvation for Spirit, Soul and Body, through Jesus Christ our Lord; in the language of the Apostles we say to you: "Grace, Mercy and Peace through the knowledge of Him who has called us to glory and virtue," and like the Apostle we thank God for every remembrance of you.

This letter is written that your hearts may rejoice and that with us you may join in gratitude and praise to God for the wonderful manifestation of His love and power, through Jesus Christ in the salvation and healing of the vast multitude who in the past year have found Him Saviour and Healer still.

Believing that very little idea exists among the people at large of the great extent and far-reaching influence of this work of God, we are giving a few facts that we know will inspire your hearts to praise.

We minister to an average of 200 people per day. Our Healing Rooms are open every weekday, which shows over 60,000 personal ministrations through prayer and laying on of hands during the past twelve months.

Fire of God

Added to these are the multitude of calls for prayer and ministration that come by telephone, telegraph, letter and cable from all parts of the world.

Ministry to the sick in their homes is another department of our work. This is accomplished by the use of two motor cars by which our ministers are conveyed from home to home, ministering to the sick who are not able to present themselves at the Healing Rooms. By these various agencies at least 100,000 ministrations are accomplished per annum.

It is that you may join with the tens of thousands thus healed of God, in common praise to "Him who has loved us, and washed us from our sins in His own blood" that these facts are set forth. Among those healed were persons suffering with cancers of every degree and character, tumors, tuberculosis, pneumonia, paralysis, diabetes, Bright's disease, and every other physical ailment.

During the flu epidemic, according to our best estimates, we ministered to not less than 3300 persons in all stages of flu and pneumonia; many of them pronounced hopeless by their physicians. And of all this great company who trusted God only and wholly, abandoning their medicines and drugs, we have only had to record one death.

Among all the agencies of healing in the known world there is no such record as this, demonstrating in the most forcible manner the effectiveness and superiority of the power of God to heal over any other known method. Proving that he who dares to trust God alone, obeying the instructions of Scripture concerning ministry in sickness, has chosen the safest, soundest and most efficient method of healing in the world.

To demonstrate the peculiar effectiveness and power of the Spirit of God over disease, we cite the following: Mrs. Wilson, S 312 Howard street, Spokane, Wash., was declared by her physicians to be suffering from internal cancer. The X-ray

John G. Lake in Spokane

showed a large abnormal growth. When ministered to by prayer and laying on of hands, the Spirit of God came powerfully upon her and in a few days the cancer loosened from her body and passed from her, both cancer and roots. Mrs. Wilson is a nurse and experienced in matters of sickness and disease, and we quote the above from her public testimony.

Many healings are instantaneous, even of the very worst forms of disease. Mr. xxxx, whose name we withhold at this time, came to the Healing Rooms on January 27th, saying: "I have just come from the offices of Dr. xxxx, where I have been examined by himself and pronounced incurable from Brights disease.

The doctor was so interested in my case that he asked permission to call in other physicians to also examine me. A group of physicians gathered about me, making a most thorough examination; when they were through the spokesman said; 'If you have anything to attend to you had better do it at once; you are going to die.' An eye specialist was then called in to examine my eyes, for on account of the extreme high blood pressure, the marvel was how I could see at all. I returned to my wife, and she persuaded me to come to the Healing Rooms, and so I have come to you. I am not interested in healing, but I want to know my Lord into whose presence I must soon enter."

We comforted him and prayed with him that he might know his Lord unto salvation; we also prayed that he might be healed. He returned on the 28th, and as we ministered to him, we said: "Forget your idea of dying; look to God with us for your healing now." As hands were laid upon him and prayer offered, the Spirit of God came upon him, causing him to tremble violently.

He returned home, ate heartily, slept soundly all night, and in the morning awoke, saying to his wife, "I feel just as good as I ever did in my life. I believe I could go to work." After examining himself and eating a hearty breakfast, he went to work and worked all day. The next morning he said, "I am going to test this matter of my healing, for every symptom of disease has apparently left me." He came downtown, went to an Old Line Life Insurance company's office and applied for a one thousand dollar policy. He was examined by the company's physicians and was passed 100 percent perfect.

These healings are of daily and hourly occurrence; still we find that few people know of their extent and power, or have little idea of the vast numbers that are being healed of the Lord.

If these were bodily healings only the results should cause all hearts to rejoice. But when we consider that great numbers of these are healed in body, soul and spirit, becoming real and intelligent Christians, manifesting their Christianity through lives of devotion and sacrifice for others, a double cause of gratitude to God is apparent.

Healings of the most violent forms of insanity, of drunkenness of evil habits, of secret vices and sins, are part and parcel of this blessed work of God.

The preaching of the Living Word in the power of God, particularly in the Masonic Temple services and the evening lecture classes has been marked throughout the year by the mighty presence of the Holy Spirit. An average of a thousand persons each week attend these services. In the public service conversions, healings, and Baptism in the Holy Spirit frequently occur, evidencing the blessed presence of the power of God.

During the year many have joined us in the purest, deepest and holiest consecration to God.

Through the Word, preached and printed, tens of thousands are reached in all parts of the country. During the

John G. Lake in Spokane

flu epidemic public services for the people of the Inland Empire were supplied by us through the medium of the Spokane daily papers.

We feel that the time has come for a great onward movement and we send a call to every lover of our Lord Jesus Christ and every lover of his fellow men to join us this year in this blessed effort for the salvation and healing of the world.

We are not spending money building church buildings and sepulchers for the dead. We use the funds entrusted to us for the immediate sending forth of this gospel of power and blessing.

If you are interested in the Living Christ, a living gospel, a real salvation and blessing of God upon sin-stricken and disease-smitten humanity, let us hear from you.

We minister to people in all parts of the world, and our correspondence daily brings the blessed tidings of wonderful deliverance from disease and death. For example: During the flu epidemic a telegram was received on a Thursday afternoon from an isolated mining camp in the mountains of Idaho, stating that one man had already died, and that 32 others in the camp were ill with flu and pneumonia, four of these already in the throes of death.

The people were assembling for our Thursday afternoon Divine Healing and Testimony meeting. At 3:30 p. m. the telegram was read to the audience with the request that all should join us in prayer, permitting the love and power of God to flow from all hearts to the stricken camp.

When prayer was concluded, a spiritual consciousness that the work had been done was evident. A second wire announced the result, followed by letters and finally by one of the number who had been healed at that moment. He related the experience of the camp as follows: About 15 minutes to

Fire of God

four o'clock in the afternoon of the day that we sent the first telegram to you, something like an electrical condition of the atmosphere took place.

Those who were suffering in a little while found that their pains had subsided or disappeared. Some were entirely healed; at once arose and dressed; others began to recover and the next morning practically the whole camp was well. The condition of the four men who were so extremely ill, changed; their suffering and choking ceased, they gave evidence of rapid recovery, and in four days were entirely well.

The world has laughed at what has been commonly termed by some as Absent Healing. Materialists have failed to comprehend the dynamic power, and the penetrative quality of the Spirit of God when applied through devotional souls whose hearts are joined with the Lord Jesus Christ in the common ministry of His Spirit.

We are endeavoring to follow the practice of our Lord and Saviour Jesus Christ, who sent forth His disciples without purse or money (see Luke 9), but anointed with the power of God to heal. We make no charges, believing that the ministry of Jesus should be without price. Love offerings are our only means of maintaining this work. We trust God to supply our every need. We invite your cooperation in the distribution of this wealth of God's love and power, praying upon your heart and life His blessing, Presence and Spirit. Your Brother and Servant in Christ Jesus,

JOHN G. LAKE, Overseer

John G. Lake in Spokane

Spokane Daily Chronicle
Sunday, April 26, 1919

The Church at Spokane
Rev. John G. Lake, Overseer

The Healing Stream

Mrs. Josephene Chant of Priest Lake, Idaho, has beautiful spiritual experiences in connection with her healing by the Lord.

My sickness began twenty years ago with a most severe breakdown. Twelve years ago I felt that I had sufficiently recovered to consider marriage and was married. However, these twelve years have been one weary drag. I have suffered almost all the time, at times my sufferings would be intense, then there would be spells of relief. What I have suffered no tongue can tell. I have doctored and doctored with many physicians without avail. This last winter life became well-neigh unbearable. I again visited Spokane and once again appealed to the physicians, only to be told there was no help for me.
Noting my sufferings and despair. A friend directed me to Rev. John G. Lake's healing rooms. I had never heard of such a thing as Divine Healing. I was unbelieving and skeptical in my mind; in fact, I had no faith in any one's ability to relieve my condition.
Mr. Lake ministered to me, laying his hands upon me. He instructed me to return every day until I was well. To me it seemed like a joke, but there was nothing else to do. There was no other hope, so I returned and was ministered to each day for several days.

Fire of God

My hair would fall out in handfuls when it was combed. One evening as I combed I involuntarily put out my hand to remove the hair from the comb, and to my surprise there was none. I looked at my comb with amazement. Then I began to examine my body. My sufferings had ceased, the terrible inflamed condition of my abdomen had disappeared and I was healed. But my mind still remained under a cloud of darkness and doubt. The next day I told Rev. Osborne of this condition. He prayed, and the following experiences came:

MRS. CHANT'S EXPERIENCE AS RELATED TO HER HUSBAND IN LETTERS

I had reached the place of development in this healing process where I had to admit that the flesh had been healed, but as yet my mind had not been touched and I could not reason the thing out. When I retired that night I prayed God that he would help me to solve the mystery. Instantly in the clouds of night, I began to see tiny motes of light, a shooting star here and there, like a radium sparkle. The starry specks gradually expanded and unfolded until on the screen a wondrous picture began to take shape, billows of clouds rolled up and parted to reveal a great light shining forth from this center in the background. This splendor increased until the clouds were all dispelled and the heavenly light only filled the sky. Slowly it began to fade like twilight creeping over, and presently was lost in the darkness. Then out of the dense darkness haloes of light began to appear and the day dawned. I looked so intently at the picture to keep it from fading out, but even as I gazed the shadows came again and the day was done. I so longed for words to convey the wondrous sight and wished that it might gleam long enough that I might ever hold it in my memory.

John G. Lake in Spokane

Like a dream of the night, you try to tell it the next morning only to find that you can not; you remember something but not clearly as in the dream. Even so it was with this halo picture. I saw it plainly, but found that I could not reproduce the rapture. Then I began to wonder whether I was awake or dreaming, and to make sure of myself I got out of bed, and walked to the bathroom, took a drink, and returned to my couch. My head had no more than touched the pillow when multitudes of angelic hosts passed before me in the sky, one by one, in a mazy, gauzy, fleecy, cloud-like sort of way, then a film came before them and hid them from view. Again and again they appeared, slowly and gracefully. No sweet tongued orator can describe, no poet express, no artist paint, no musician sing or play the harmony vibrating and radiating from those forms. Oh, that they might stand before me forever. I prayed but even as I prayed they vanished and I saw them no more. All night long it was one beautiful transfiguration after another and when morning came and I looked out upon nature it all had a different meaning; there was something there I had never seen before and that something was God. This impression stayed with me all day. I felt as though some wonderful change was going to take place in me, some latent power stored up in me was going to break loose — like the Falls of Niagara, whose power nothing could resist — like a mighty earthquake, changing the whole face of the earth — like all the war demons of Europe turned loose and consumed as by fire, leaving only peace on Flanders fields — like lightning from above striking me and flashing forth the electric spark to others — as though a word from my lips and a touch from my hand would open the eyes of the blind, unstop the ears of the deaf, bid sickness of every form scatter. I prayed that power might be given me to heal sinful, suffering humanity. Why can I write thus? I am putting forth no mental effort whatever, but some impelling force just pushes my hand

Fire of God

and writes the words. It is the finger of God. The mists are clearing and God is transforming my mind.

Mind Pictures

These words come to me, "Write what thou seest in a book, for this is your mission and for this you were born."

Centuries ago King Solomon prayed that God would give him an understanding, and he received what he asked for and much more. One all-consuming power I have craved all my life and that is that I might be able to express in words what I felt was in me. So now I prayed that God would heal the diseased condition of the cells of my brain so that I would have clear understanding. While I prayed I felt that the request was granted before my lips formed the words and I knew for a certainty that the Spirit of God had begun operating on my brain. Instantly something seemed to cut loose and layers and layers of pressure were lifted from my head, and a peace of mind infinitely soothing stole gently over me, and I felt like a babe being lulled to sleep on the mother's breast. All the way home that afternoon I kept singing softly over and over again. "Shine on me, even me: let thy radiance shine on me." Then the blessings started to pour into my soul faster than I could receive them and I asked God to increase the container. Then another electric wave would thrill me, and so it continued all afternoon. Night came on. Oh, what a night! A thousand years would not be long enough to tell the mind experiences. It seemed to me that every ennobling and sublime thought ever conceived by man lashed through my mind and I was able to discern the mind behind the creations of art, whether book or picture. I put my fingers to my eyes, trying to see the thought, to my ears to hear it, to my nose to catch the fragrance, to my hair to radiate the beauty, to my fingertips to properly shape the thought, and last of all to my tongue to say the words. I had

John G. Lake in Spokane

grasped the thought but found that I lacked the power to express it, and so when morning came this vision passed from my memory, as had all the others, but this time instead of leaving clouds there was a pure white light, and I named it "The Light of Love, the Soul Touch." Then this mental picture developed: God is the artist, with all power of expression; the face of Christ the perfect picture; the Holy Spirit, the paint; the hand of man, the brush to apply the color to produce the proper light and shade effects on me, the white canvas. As yet there is nothing but the white screen. The sanctified touch of God's love must possess and thrill me until the face of Christ appears, the picture that will never fade away. I can not express God alright until God is incarnate in me, then the unity of the Father, Son and Holy Spirit will shine forth in my body, soul and spirit. The kiss of almighty love will be implanted on my brow, for God is love. This oneness with God I desire and he will gratify the craving through Christ by the power of the Holy Spirit, then will the unbroken speech of God, the Word of God, be expressed or manifested in me in its fullness. The day is not yet done, the medium of expression is not yet healed, but I am confident that God will accomplish his design in me so that I may go forth in the power of his might and Love to fulfill my mission.

MRS. JOSEPHINE CHANT

Fire of God

Spokane Daily Chronicle, Spokane, WA
Sat., May 3, 1919

The Old-Time Religion

The phrase "Old Time Religion," is familiar to us all, did you ever inquire how old? As old as Abraham, who prayed for the wives of Abimelech and they were healed. As old as Moses, who prayed a famous prayer in seven words for his sister Miriam, who was a leper, white as snow, and God healed her. As old as Elisha, who prayed for a double portion of the spirit of God that rested on his tutor Elijah, and it was given him. As old as Daniel, whose faith in the living God closed the mouths of the lions. As old as Isaiah, who prophesied of the coming of Jesus and of a Kingdom of Christ yet to come. As old as Jesus, who revealed the perfect Will of God, teaching in their synagogues, preaching the gospel of the Kingdom and healing all manner of sickness and all manner of disease among the people. As old as the Apostles, who healed them every one. As old as Philip, a Holy Ghost anointed Christian, who did many signs and wonders. As old as Paul, who became a disciple and Apostle of Jesus many days after the crucifixion, resurrection, ascension and glorification of the Lord, who healed the sick and raised the dead. As old as Thecia of Athens, to whom multitudes of sick made pilgrimages and they were healed by the power of God. As old as St. Francis of Assisi, who likewise ministered the virtue of the Risen Christ to the sick and sinful and healed them. As old as John Wesley, who declared that the prayer of faith was the only system of physic known to the early church for four hundred years.

John G. Lake in Spokane

As old as Edward Lion, a native of Africa, who still lives and under whose ministry tens of thousands of sick have been healed of the Lord.

The same Gospel, the same knowledge of the living God, the same power of the spirit, reached Mrs. Oscar G. Gilbertson of N 4115 Helena street, Spokane, whose body was so intensely relaxed through disease that her hip came out of joint, whose suffering was so intense that as the Rev. Lake prayed for her, kneeling at her bedside, his soul was so overcome by her agony the prayer was rendered ineffectual. Returning to the healing rooms he called the other ministers to join in prayer. A group of them bowed their heads, reached forth to God in faith, believing that the Spirit of God through the soul of Jesus and through their own hearts applied to the suffering body of the tortured woman, would make her whole, found it so and the limb was restored to its socket.

Men have called it absent healing. We call it present power. The power of God applied through the holy desire to bless and heal a needy fellow creature. The Divine secret that has baffled the wise and mystified the philosophers. The living present Holy Spirit of God, Jesus Christ "The same yesterday and today and forever."

Our Sunday public services are held in the Knights of Pythias Castle, corner of Riverside and Jefferson. The morning service at 11: a. m. and afternoon service at 3 p. m.

Our Healing Rooms are at 340 Rookery building, where we minister every week day to the sick and sorrowful in the name of the Lord Jesus Christ, from 10 a.m. until 4 p.m.
If you are in need of blessing or assistance, call us, our telephone is Main 1463

Fire of God

Christian Baptism and Kingdom Consecration
Sermon Delivered by JOHN G. LAKE, Overseer

> **Christian Baptism**
> AND
> **Kingdom Consecration**
> Sermon Delivered By
> **JOHN G. LAKE**
> Overseer
> PUBLISHED BY
> ZION APOSTOLIC CHURCH
> SPOKANE, WASH.
> PRICE 25 CENTS

PERSONAL EXPERIENCE IS PRICELESS

Personal Christian experience is the basis of all religious faith. I am thinking just now of old Jacob, who had been looking after his father-in-law's cattle for fourteen years. He was a shrewd fellow and a real old Jew. He had been practicing a law of suggestion on his father-in-laws cattle, until he practically owned the herd. When they were to separate and Jacob had his things and started down the road, I guess his father-in-law thought he had about all there was on the farm. He also started down the road and overtook Jacob, and in the course of conversation Jacob said,
"I KNOW BY EXPERIENCE THAT THE LORD HATH

John G. Lake in Spokane

BLESSED ME." No doubt about it. He had the cattle. He was in possession of the herd.

So personal experience is the great basis of all faith and growth in God. It is good and blessed to see what God does with others and for others, but the only satisfying thing, and the only thing that satisfies your own nature is that which God accomplished within your own heart, and that which you yourself are cognizant of, whether it be in Salvation, Sanctification, Consecration, Christian Baptism, Baptism of the Spirit, or any other Christian experiences.

THE ORDINANCE OF BAPTISM

It has been a great joy to me in these few years to realize that God is revealing once again, by the Holy Ghost, the real revelation of the purpose of the Ordinances that Jesus Christ established, particularly the Ordinance of Baptism. This ordinance, in the beginning of the Church's history, was a great and blessed and dignified ordinance of God, which caused men and women to come deliberately forward and commit themselves to the Lord as disciples of Jesus, notwithstanding that the mere fact of that deed meant that their names would be taken by a Roman officer. Speaking now of the time of the great and terrible persecution of the Christians after Christ, and which continued until the Third Century.

BAPTISMAL CONSECRATION

I am looking forward and rejoicing in the return of the old-time Christianity, and note that when the Holy Ghost began to move afresh in these latter days, he brought back the old-time spirit of real sacrifices, not only the giving up of that which a man possesses, but the giving up of himself, and entire committing of himself, to the Lord his God. And this is the point that I want to speak to you about this afternoon. A real

Fire of God

Kingdom Consecration of all you have and all you are, — property and person, Body and Soul and Spirit to Christ and the Kingdom.

PRESENTATION
The presentation of ourselves to God, was the great original fundamental issue that underlaid the whole subject of Baptism in the beginning, when Jesus gave the command that constituted Christian Baptism; for there is only one command in the entire Word of God that constitutes Christian Baptism, and gives instruction as to its mode.

COMMAND
Now you notice what I say, that there is ONLY ONE COMMAND IN THE ENTIRE WORD OF GOD THAT GIVES INSTRUCTIONS CONCERNING CHRISTIAN BAPTISM AND ITS MODE. No other command deals with the mode of baptism, — just that one command in Matthew 28:19, given by the Lord Himself.

MODE
Coming from the Lord, it is absolutely official and binding, not to be discussed or disputed, but OBEYED. Indeed, this was His final command, here He was borne upward by the power of God as He stood on the Mount of Olives about to be separated from the disciples. He said to them:: "Go ye therefore, and teach all nations, baptizing them INTO The name of the Father, AND of the Son AND of the Holy Ghost."

MEANING
One of the blessed things I feel the Lord is laying on our hearts today is a return to that ancient practice and mode of Baptism, instituted by Christ, practiced by the apostles and the Church officially for eight hundred years, or until the official

introduction of single immersion by the edict of Pope Greggory. Not only in the name OF, or by the authority of, but there is an inner meaning, a better one. Into the NATURE of, into the CHARACTER of, into the LIFE OF THE Father, AND of the Holy Ghost. Baptism is not an act of obedience. It is ten thousand times more. It is an induction into the nature and character and the life of God the Father and God the Son and God the Holy Ghost. In other words, induct them into the life of the Father, induct them into the life of the Son, induct them into the life of the Holy Ghost.

BAPTISM INTO THE FATHER

Therefore, in the life of the individual who has been baptized into the NATURE of the Father, of necessity there must come forth the characteristics of the Father-heart, the great Father quality that loves its offspring, that gives itself for the children, that stands in strength and sacrifice, in dignity and power, to guard the interests of the Household. "Into the name of the Father," Into the NATURE OF THE FATHER. That wonderful Fatherhood, that reaches out and yearns to produce, and reproduce, itself in mankind. So God the Father is yearning to reproduce Himself in us, — in you. In me.

BAPTISM INTO THE SON

The climax of salvation is the reproduction in the human family of the Christ of God, the real Christ of God reproduced in you, in me, as members of the great whole. Just as Jesus Himself was the reproduction of the Father, so the collective Body of Christ, the Church, is the reproduction of Christ in the world.

"Baptizing them into the NATURE of the Son," into the sacrifice of the Son, who gave Himself; the Son who died even that we might live. The Son who yielded Himself unto death,

Fire of God

in order that the life which He gave forth might be transplanted into the human nature and mind. That is the great purpose of the Gospel, the REPRODUCTION of the Christ, the Son of God, in the family, the Body, the Saints, the Bride of Christ.

Beloved, it is my conviction that the time has come when from the Body of Christ, or Church, from the Bride of Christ, who is the chosen of Christ, there shall come forth that which the Scripture portrays, the Man child, or one born out of the Bride, just as Jesus was born out of the Virgin, filled with power and dignity and purity. Not an individual, but a COMPANY of the saints of God, who are born to rule; to whom God has given by the Spirit ability to govern. Who will be partakers and rulers with the Lord Himself, in His Kingdom on earth.

BAPTISM INTO THE HOLY GHOST

Once again, there is a phase of Baptism that you and I have commonly not recognized. "Baptizing them into the Holy Ghost." As Jesus uttered that command, as He stood on the Mount of Olives, He included a name, the HOLY GHOST, into which no man had been baptized before. We see the Fatherhood of God, we recognize the Sonship of God, the Word speaks to us about the HOUSEHOLD of God, but we fail to recognize the characteristics of the SPIRIT of God.

These are the characteristics of MOTHERHOOD. The Spirit that broods, the spirit that yearns, the spirit that endeavors to draw us back to God, the spirit that reaches forth, that hovers over us, that sustains, that blesses, that comforts, that guides, that controls.

So we see the family of God: The Fatherhood of God, the Motherhood of God, the Sonship of God, The Household of God.

So in the life of the real Christian, there should, there

MUST BE APPARENT IN OUR CHARACTER, THE CHARACTER-ISTICS OF THE Triune God. There should be evidence, that inborn in the Christian, are the God-qualities of construction creation, character building, cementing the Mind of God that every one, who by the blood of Jesus is admitted to membership in the Body of Christ, should reproduce in OTHERS the qualities that God has planted in them. Blessed be His precious name!

FOLLOWING HIS EXAMPLE

Beloved, you and I as sons of God by virtue of our sins having been washed away, after we have yielded ourselves to God, stand before mankind to present ourselves to the Lord, even as Jesus Himself presented Himself to God, a complete consecration,
"UNTO ALL RIGHTEOUSNESS."

THE GREAT BLUNDER

Now may I call your attention to one thing? The question of baptism has usually been presented to the world from the Sixth of Romans, which in itself is not a discussion of Baptism at all. The subject of Baptism in the Sixth of Romans is only used as an illustration of the deeper DEATH-LIFE of the Christian. NO MENTION IS MADE WHATEVER OF BAPTISM EITHER INTO THE FATHER, OR THE SPIRIT. PAUL DEALS ONLY WITH DEATH OF SIN. THE SUBJECT HE WAS EMPHASIZING, WHICH IS DEMONSTRATED IN OUR ONE IMMERSION, INTO THE SON, WHILE JESUS COMMANDED AN IMMERSION INTO EACH SEPARATE NAME OF THE TRINITY. Paul's teaching all the way through is filled with the subject of the death-life of the Christian.

For years and years, as I have gone into the Word of

Fire of God

God, and prayed over these questions, and heard men teach on the subject of baptism, there was something in my spirit that always revolted against the CROSS-DEATH being taught as the Christian's death. The cross-death is the death of the old man, and our sins are nailed to the cross, and are done with.

Therefore, the man who comes to present himself for Baptism, ought to be considered, and should consider and reckon himself as finished with sin. It is past, and done, and gone, and now he stands before the world to present himself as one who is finished with sin in all its aspects. He presents himself as a saved man, that he may come forth a new man in Christ Jesus, declaring himself for evermore committed unto God the Father, unto God the Son, unto God the Holy Ghost.

THE TYPE

In going into this question of the death-life, my spirit recently has been drawn out to observe that in the Old Testament, there is a type and evidence of the real DEATH LIFE. In the Sixteenth of Leviticus we have that wonderful picture of the Atonement and LIFE-DEATH of the Lord; likewise the Atonement and LIFE-DEATH of His people, in the presentation of the two goats to represent the LIFE-DEATH and physical CROSS-DEATH of the Lord. The one goat was to be slain; its blood to be sprinkled on behalf of the people; its body to be burned, consumed and destroyed without the camp.

THE LIFE-DEATH

The one goat, the one I especially want to call your attention to now, is the one that was taken on the tow rope, by a Levite, three days into the barren sands of the Wilderness, until worn and weary of exhaustion and starvation it was left to die. This was the other phase of sacrifice — not the giving of its blood and the burning of its body, but the working out of

John G. Lake in Spokane

God in its own being, until IN REAL LIFE IT DIES.

JESUS ON THE TOW ROPE

We come to the life of the Lord Jesus Christ, who presented Himself at the River Jordan, that ALL the RIGHTEOUSNESS OF GOD might be FULFILLED in Him, and immediately following, we read that HE was DRAVE or led by the Spirit into the Wilderness, to be tempted by the devil. We see that after His Baptism, He was under the control of the Spirit of God. Being under control of the Spirit of God, just like the goat that was led by the Levite, so our Jesus by the Holy Ghost, God's Levite, was lead three days. God's time, which is three years (a day for a year) into the Wilderness, just as the original goat had been led, until He died out to the claims of his three-fold nature. For three years, not by the **death of the cross,** but by a LIVING-DEATH, the yielding of Himself moment by moment, hour by hour, day by day, unto His Father's will, He demonstrated to God and man that He was an Overcomer, and was the one man who had triumphed over SIN and over SELF.

THE RESULT

Thus, HE BECAME THE AUTHOR of Eternal Salvation, and so our Christ, our Lord, could come and present Himself at the cross as the second goat for destruction of the body that His physical life might be poured out, that His blood might be shed for the salvation of man.

NEED OF PROPER TEACHING

Beloved, let me tell you, there has been a superficiality in our dealings with men. We say, "Brother, come and kneel at the altar and die, and yield yourself on the cross," etc, and the individual comes and he finds that when he goes away that the operation of death has not taken place in him, as he had desired. Beloved, we have been calling the people's attention largely to the wrong figure. There is something that goes before presenting ourselves for destruction on the cross. It is the presentation of the man himself unto God in his three-fold being, just as Jesus Himself presented Himself at the River Jordan in His three-fold nature unto God; then immediately following went into the Wilderness, where a three-fold temptation appealing to the separate portions of His own being, was immediately presented to Him, and rejected by our Lord.

TRIUNE GOD, TRIUNE MAN

We stand before you, as you already recognize, a triune being, even as God Himself is triune. God the Father, God the Son, and God the Holy Ghost. You and I as men, by the Word of God, are likewise triune. "I pray God," says the apostle, "that your whole spirit, and soul, and body be preserved entire, without blame, unto the coming of our Lord."

MAN'S TRINITY DEFINED

May I define in a word our spirit, our soul, our body. OUR BODY is our animal consciousness, our being and life. OUR SOUL is our self, or sense-consciousness, by which all our five senses are moved, and operated and understood. In other words, our ego, our self, our mind, our sense-life. It is our sense-consciousness. Again OUR SPIRIT is the divine in us, by which we know God; by which we test things which are spiritual; by which we commune with our Lord and Saviour Jesus Christ. It is our God-consciousness. Each department of our being is to be presented to the living God in a real Baptism. Blessed be His precious name!

John G. Lake in Spokane

DESIRE
    I trust, therefore, that these dear ones who have already arranged to be baptized, and those who will arrange to be baptized, may be permitted to come to that baptism with a new understanding of the claims of God on them, and a new preparedness to yield our being — Body and Soul and Spirit unto God.

RECKONED HIMSELF DEAD
    Jesus so yielded Himself. Therefore immediately after His yielding, standing before God, standing before mankind, He reckoned Himself dead in all the departments of His being, in His Spirit, in His Soul, in His Body, to the claims of His own nature — wholly yielded unto God.

TEMPTING THE BODY
    Then just as the goat, who yielded himself to the control of the Levite, and was taken on the tow rope, three days into the Wilderness to die, so Jesus was led by the Spirit into the Wilderness. Mind you, He was LED by the SPIRIT. He did not get there by accident. It was in the purpose of God that He should be tested and tried, in order to demonstrate that His Consecration was genuine and in God. The temptation begins. First Satan presents to Him a temptation peculiar to the demands of the body alone. He had fasted forty days and forty nights, and "was an hungered." God says so, Satan says, "Command that these stones be made bread." But Jesus our Lord remembered that at the Jordan He had committed His BODY, and all its claims, unto God, and rejected the temptation and put it from Him by the Word of God. God's glory and man's salvation were more to Him than the hunger calls of His BODY. Bless God

TEMPTING THE SOUL

Once again, Satan seeing that temptation had failed, makes a claim to the higher realm of his nature, His mind or soul. He takes Him to a pinnacle of the temple, and says, "Cast thyself down" before these unbelieving Jews, so that they seeing you are able to cast yourself from such a height, will recognize you as their Prince, and crown you as King. It is all right, do not be afraid, "He will give His angels charge over you to keep you in all your ways." But our Jesus, remembering that He had committed His self-life, His SOUL, His mind unto God, rejected the temptation; the Tempter is turned aside. No crossless crowning for the Lord. No bloodless glory for the Lord. He had committed Himself to God. God had given Him as a ransom for many. He, the Father, gave His only begotten Son, so there was no way for our Lord to go but to go the way the Father had mapped out. Jesus knew no will of his own — only the Father's will. Bless God

How abundantly this is demonstrated in the Garden of Gethsemane, when the great climax of that great earth-life, or that DEATH-LIFE HAD ARRIVED. Jesus went into the Garden, when the sorrows of mankind, or consciousness of sin, came upon Him with such abundant power that from His person there began to flow great drops of blood, falling down unto the ground. Reason, science, everything, demonstrates that when such a thing becomes possible that death is very near.

I knew a man who sweat blood. For a time, about three months, blood would ooze out of his pores, and when he would awake his pillow would be dotted with blood, because of the tremendous burden of sorrow that he then lived under. That was Judge xxxx of, xxxx during Dr. Dowie's breakdown. His wife told me that for three months she would have to put a napkin over his pillow. Beloved, I tell you there are some hearts, there are some lives, that feel the sorrows of man.

John G. Lake in Spokane

Reason, everything, demonstrates that when such a thing in any measure becomes possible in a human life, that death is apparent. In the case of our Lord it was not a little drop or two, but the great drops of blood oozed from His person, so that the Lord Himself, understanding and knowing and being convinced that even His life was passing out, prayed that wonderful prayer in the Garden. "Lord, if it be possible, let this cup pass from Me." Jesus was not a coward. He was not praying for fear of the cross. Instead, He was a hero. He was praying in an agony of fear that He would not reach the cross. God had designed what His end should be, and He by the consent of His own nature, for you and me, had likewise designed that there could only be one end, and that was that He should die on the cross. His prayer was heard. Angels came and strengthened Him, and then with joy and gladness our Lord went on to the cross, and poured out His life's blood.

So we see the temptation to cast Himself from the pinnacle of the temple, making an exhibition of His power, and thereby getting the acclaim of mankind, was not God's way, nor God's will. He had committed His being, His mind, His soul to God. He could not go that way, and He did not.

TEMPTING THE SPIRIT

Once again, He has committed His spirit unto God. Satan realizing that the appeal to the animal consciousness of the man had failed, realizing that the appeal to His mind, His soul, His reason had failed, presents a new temptation, a spiritual one. He says, "Now Jesus look," And by a supernatural power Jesus is permitted in a glance, in a moment of time, "to see all the Kingdoms of the world, and the glory of them." He did not miss any of them. That spiritual vision of the Lord reached forth and saw "all the Kingdoms of the earth,

Fire of God

and the glory of them." Then Satan said, "Jesus, all these will I give thee if thou wilt fall down and worship me.."

But bless God, Jesus had committed at the River Jordan unto ALL the will of God. He could not worship at the feet of the devil, nor acknowledge him Ruler. This LIFE-DEATH and His reliance on the Word of God gave victory. He spurned the temptation and the Tempter, and went God's way, His own choice likewise, to the bloody cross.

Men have magnified the sacrifice of the cross, but have minimized or have failed to see the magnitude of the victory attained by Jesus in His LIFE-DEATH of three years, which left His Body, His Soul, His Spirit so completely surrendered to all the will of God that the cross, the death of the body, was but a fitting climax.

Therefore our Christ, having committed His spirit unto God, rejected the temptation of the devil, and started from that hour to demonstrate by His daily life, and His daily living, that He was DEAD to ALL the claims of His Nature. Thus He could say, "The words that I speak, they are spirit, and they are life." "The works that I do, I do not of myself, but the Father that dwelleth in Me, He doeth works." "I came not to do mine own will, but the will of Him that sent me."

Bless God! There was one life surrendered unto God. The only life in all the race of man that was able to present itself unto God, obedient even unto death; death to every part of His nature, His SPIRIT, His SOUL. His BODY. Blessed be the name of Jesus!

GOD'S DESIGN

Beloved, God has designed for you and me that same blessed wonderful, triune consecration, typified in a Triune Baptism, into the NATURE of the Father, AND INTO THE

John G. Lake in Spokane

NATURE OF THE SON, AND into the nature of the Holy Ghost.

When these dear ones who are to be baptized go down into the water, let it be with this consciousness, that you have committed yourself, your Body, your Soul, your Spirit unto God. That you voluntarily take the hand of the Spirit of God, to be led into the Wilderness, or out of the Wilderness, on the tow rope of the Holy Ghost, whithersoever He leads. Bless God.

HOLY GHOST CONVICTION

I believe in Triune Immersion. There is no doubt about it. I believe as any honest student can see, that the teaching of single immersion is only a partial revelation of the wonderful subject of baptism.

Triune Immersion is the Holy Ghost revelation of the subject. It is according to the Word of God, and the only form of baptism according to the Word of God. Everywhere I go I find that God is revealing this fact to the saints, the real ones. The superficial may continue to baptize by other modes, but the real Kingdom Christian will find satisfaction and gratification and consciousness of full obedience only in fulfilling the ENTIRE COMMAND OF THE Lord Jesus Christ. **It is the end of all discussion on the subject of baptism.** Christians who have been baptized by single immersion are convicted of the truthfulness of Triune Immersion, because of its greater truth and fuller obedience. But no man, having been baptized by triune immersion could be convicted of single immersion, except he be a fool, no more than one having been immersed once, could be convicted of the need of being sprinkled.

I am looking forward to the day when the Church of God will recognize that they have robbed mankind of one of the most glorious privileges of the Christian life, that of a clear,

Fire of God

definite committing of all their triune being unto a triune God, that a triune operation may take place in the heart — death to sin, life to God, and power for service. Yea more that you commit yourself even unto death, as Jesus did, your body, your soul, your spirit, that when Satan appears to tempt you, as he will, you will be able to say even as the Lord did, and as the Lord showed by His action, that your triune being is committed unto God, and you refuse the offers of Satan, because you belong to God. Yea more. THAT THE ALL THINGS OF EVERY DAY, AND THE EVERY THING OF EACH DAY, may be the means by which your life is demonstrated to be in the hands of God, and that you are yielded body and soul and spirit unto Him.

EMPHASIS

Permit me to emphasize this fact, that the disciples baptized men according to the command of the Lord. When Paul dealt with the death-life of the Christian, in the Sixth of Romans, he used the subject of baptism (into Jesus Christ) as an illustration, singling out the one act from a complete triune baptism, the one that best illustrated the subject he was discussing. He said, "You baptized into His death," into the death of Christ, "that like as He was raised up, so you too shall be raised up to the life of purity, holiness, virtue and truth. God Bless you.

SCHOLASTIC AUTHORITY

Recently I had the great pleasure of visiting with Dr. Kolvoord, the eminent Dutch scholar and authority on technical interpretations of Scripture, a scholar of scholars and teacher of teachers. Dr. Kolvoord has been a Baptist all his life, practicing single immersion. My beloved friend and brother in Christ, Archibald Fairley, in discussing with him the subject of baptism, in the great commission of Mat. 28:19-20, asked him to analyze the words "baptizing them" from the Greek, saying to him, "I believe you will find, as I have, that the words meant to immerse REPEATEDLY," for the Greek word used is not the word *Bapto*, to immerse, but *baptizo*, to IMMERSE REPEATEDLY.

Dr. Kolvoord examined it in the literal Greek, then in the classical. At the conclusion he said to Bro. Fairley, "I am amazed. You are right." And Bro. Fairley said, "Now, Brother, you have seen the truth. How about it?"

So we rejoice that the illumination of the Holy Ghost makes clear to the Spirit makes clear many things that the profoundest minds have failed to see, and though the unilluminated still continue to practice baptism by single immersion, some even by sprinkling, again we rejoice that God through the Holy Ghost is establishing world-wide, a real Kingdom Triune Baptism, into the name of the Father, and of the Son, and of the Holy Ghost — three immersions, constituting one baptism. Amen.

A CONVERSATION

Desiring all possible light on this Spirit of God, I asked for the privilege of a conversation with that God-anointed prophet of the Lord, Brother Archibald Fairley, which was as follows:

QUESTION

DR. LAKE: Brother, the common understanding of the subject of Baptism is single immersion. When Jesus said, "Baptizing them into the name of the Father, and of the Son, and of the Holy Ghost" people fail to see what the Greek really indicates, that it was to be a repetition of immersions. Instead, they simply apply it in a separate manner, as though Jesus was speaking to a multitude of people, and that each was to be baptized. Won't you let me have your explanation of how the Greek shows that to be a repetition of immersions?

GOD'S ANSWER
GIVEN BY THE HOLY GHOST IN THE SPIRIT OF PROPHECY

FAIRLEY: The Spirit of the Lord gives me this. First of all the purpose of Christian immersion is that in the act we enter into the death of our Lord Jesus Christ. That His three-fold nature was a reflex of the God-nature, God the Father, God the Son and God the Holy Ghost, taking possession of His three-fold human nature, after it was subjected. This immersion into the name of the Father, and of the Son and of the Holy Ghost, was a three-fold immersion, and typifies the death of the natural spirit, the seat of God-consciousness, dead, that it may become the seat of Christ-consciousness. And that we in like manner, judge our body, the seat of animal-consciousness, the Temple of the Divine Spirit. Thus the God-nature was revealed in the God-man, covering His human nature after He made consecration, the consecration of the immersion in the Jordan.

Therefore, Matthew 28:19 means this: Baptizing them INTO the NATURE of the Father, AND of the Son, AND of the Holy Ghost. The act of immersion is that act whereby I reckon my human nature dead, my spirit dead to the working of the human spirit, and open to the working of the Divine Spirit; and the flesh, my soul, dead to the working of the self life, and open to the working of the Jesus life, and my body really dead, first in that determines health, and open to the power of the Holy Ghost in the flesh. So I determine the health of my body, not by the evidence of healthy blood, but by the power of the Holy Ghost working in me, as He worked in the Christ to raise

John G. Lake in Spokane

Him from the dead, and set Him above all principalities and powers on the Throne with God.

The great fight in the future, and this side of the glory scene, will be for the possession of the body. Not I believe that this body will be glorified, but that the flesh will be the scene of conflict. That the sons of the Most High, who are to take the Kingdom, the inner Kingdom first, must walk by faith and not by sight. Must take their stand in His health, not as they feel it, not the evidence of their five senses, but must believe the record of God's Word. Since they have made a three-fold consecration in the way before mentioned, their LIFE is truly hid with Christ in God. In Christ in God, in the victorious Christ, the Man on the Throne, in the place of DOMINION where the forces of the enemy are under His feet. This is the victory, even our faith.

The overcomer must begin to walk by faith, and not by sight. He must reckon upon the life that now is in His Lord, in His Head, and not what his five senses bring to him of life for the emotion of life through the blood.

DR LAKE: Bro. Fairley, what causes the difference of opinion, and various interpretations of the same Scripture?

FAIRLEY: Every man who interprets Scripture is biased by his size in God, by his experience in the God-life.

DR. LAKE: In my judgment that is what causes discussion on the subject of Triune Immersion. Really the persons who see only single immersion, have not got the size in God, or illumination of the Spirit sufficient to use the depth and power of God's Work; to see what God teaches.

FAIRLEY: They believe in the death that occurs in a moment or a day, but not a death that begins now and never ends until the revelation of Christ in the air.

The immersion spoken of in Mat. 28:19 is that act that begins by the subjection of my life to God and ends in my being part of the ruling God in the Age to come. The best figure to use to cover our relationship with the Christ, is the figure of the Bride and Bridegroom. The Bride has lived her simple, carefree life from babyhood, but from the moment she becomes known to the world by her other name, she professes that she is ONE IN NATURE WITH HER Bridegroom, one in everything with him.

Thus throughout the New Testament, the words, "in the name of," the Holy Ghost speaking to those who desire to be the Bride class, really means into the name, or rather into the NATURE OF THE Christ, of God's Anointed, of the Man Jesus, who at the Jordan offered Himself unto ALL THE WILL OF God, and became the Christ, or God's Anointed. The Bride is the wife of God's Anointed. Therefore, she is of the anointed class, the offered-up class, the poured-out class. She enters from the moment of her betrothal, of her offering herself up in a true immersion, into the nature of her Lord; sharing His burden, which He now has on the Throne for a lost world. The effect of this sharing His burden is that His nature displeases her nature, and bit by bit the passion of His love for man Possess her, and her life is poured out for the lost world.

John G. Lake in Spokane

Copyright applied for

**We minister to the World
Distance is not barrier
Write us**

"Not by might nor by power;
But by my Spirit,
Saith the Lord of Hosts."

> We minister to the World
> Distance is no barrier.
> Write us.
>
> "Not by might nor by power;
> But by my Spirit,
> Saith the Lord of Hosts."

Fire of God

The Spokesman-Review
Sunday Morning, September 14, 1919

Zion Apostolic Church

The Southern Association of Evangelists have written to us as follows:

Rev. John G. Lake
Spokane, Washington

Dear Sir:

We are submitting the following questions to about twenty-five of the leading professors, preachers and evangelists for reply, and recognizing your extensive experience in the ministry of healing, trust you will favor us with an early reply.
1. Is God able to heal?
2. Does God ever heal?
3. Does God always heal?
4. Does God use means in healing?

Articles answering questions 1,2, and 3 have already appeared in the columns of the Spokesman Review. We now present article four, replying to question four. "Does God use means in healing?"

By the term "means" is understood the varied remedies, medicines and potions commonly used by the world at large as prescribed for the sick. In short, materia medica.

This should be an extremely easy question for any one to decide. The world has always had her systems of healing. They were the thousand and one systems of healing evolved in

John G. Lake in Spokane

all the centuries. They are as old as the human race. They were mankind's endeavor to alleviate suffering. They existed in the days of Jesus just as they exist today.

Systems of so-called healing are without number. The ancient Egyptians used them and were apparently as proficient in the practice of the same as our modern physicians. Indeed, their knowledge of chemistry seems to have superceded ours, as they were able to produce an embalming substance that preserved the human body and kept it from dissolution, and almost every museum of note has its samples of Egyptian mummies.

It is the unintelligent who suppose that the ancient physicians were any less skillful in the healing of the sick through their means, remedies and systems than is the modern physician of our own day. Of the supposed curative value of our modern medical practice there is an abundance of testimony from the very heads of the medical profession that should be sufficient to convince any candid thinker of their valuelessness. The public commonly believe that medicine is a great science, and that its practice is entirely scientific. Whereas, so great a man in the forefront of his profession as Professor Douglas McClaggen, who occupied the chair of Medical Jurisprudence in the University of Edinburgh, Scotland, declared: "There is no such thing as the science of medicine. From the days of Hippocrates and Galen until now we have been stumbling in the dark, from diagnosis to diagnosis, from treatment to treatment and have not found the first stone on which to found medicine as a science."

While Dr. James Mason Good of London, England, who was so eminent in his profession that for twenty five years he had in his care the royal house of Britain, declared his convictions before the British Medical association in these words: "The science of medicine is founded upon conjecture

Fire of God

and improved by murder. Our medicines have destroyed more lives than all the wars, pestilence and famines combined."

The famous Professor Chauss of Germany states with emphasis: "The common use of medicine for the curing of disease is unquestionably highly detrimental and destructive and in my judgement is an agent for the creation of disease rather than its cure, in that there is continuously set up in the human system abnormal conditions more detrimental to human life than the disease from which the patient is suffering.

Our own Dr. Holmes of Boston, formerly president of the Massachusetts Medical association, said in an address before the Massachusetts Medical association: "It is my conviction, after practicing medicine for thirty-five years, that if the whole materia medica were cast into the bottom of the sea it would be all the better for mankind and all the worse for the fishes."

From these quotations by the great heads of medical profession in varied countries, we perceive the power of the Word of God which declares: "In vain shall they use many medicines. There is no healing for thee there."

Dr. John B. Murphy, the greatest surgeon our country has produced, has spoken his mind concerning SURGERY as follows: " Surgery is a confession of helplessness. Being unable to assist the diseased organ, we remove it. If I had my life to live over again I would endeavor to discover preventative medicine, in the hope of saving the organ instead of destroying it."

Just prior to his death, he wrote an article entitled, "The Slaughter of the Innocents," condemning cutting out of tonsils and adenoids, demonstrating that the presence of inflammation and pus and the consequent enlargement was due to secretion in the system that found lodgement in the tonsils and that the removal of the tonsils in no way remedied the difficulty, the

John G. Lake in Spokane

poison being generated in the system. And he purposed to give his knowledge to the public for their protection from useless operations that he regarded as criminal.

God's Way In Contrast To Man's Way

What then, did Jesus have in mind as better than the world's systems of healing, which He never used or countenanced? God's remedy is a person, not a thing. The remedy that Jesus ministered to the sick was a spiritual one. It was the Holy Spirit of God. The tangible, living quality and nature of the living God, ministered through the soul and hands of Jesus Christ to the sick one.

So conscious was the woman who was healed of the issue of blood that she had received the remedy, and of its effect and power in her, upon only touching the hem of His garment, that she "felt in her body that she was made whole of that plague." Jesus likewise was aware of the transmission of the healing power, for He said: "Some one hath touched me, for I perceive that virtue has gone out of me."

This same virtue was ministered through the hands of the apostles and of the seventy. Also of the early Christians, when they received from God through the Holy Ghost the ability to minister the Spirit of God to others. Of the twelve apostles it is said, "He gave them power and authority over all devils, and to cure diseases. And He sent them to preach the kingdom of God, and to heal the sick." (Luke 9:1,2)

Of the seventy it is written: "He sent them two by two into every city and place whither He himself would come, and said unto them, Heal the sick that are therein, and say unto them, the kingdom of God is come nigh unto you."

So vital was this living Spirit of God and its healing virtue in the lives of the early Christians that it is recorded of Paul that they brought handkerchiefs and aprons to him, that

Fire of God

they might touch his body, and when these were laid upon the sick they were healed and the demons went out of them.
(Acts 19) In this instance even inanimate objects, handkerchiefs and aprons were receptacles for the Spirit of God imparted to them from the Holy Spirit filled person of the apostle Paul.

This was not an experience for the early Christian alone, but is the common experience of men and women everywhere who have dared to disbelieve the devil's lie, so carefully fostered and proclaimed by the church at large, that the days of miracles are past.

Every advanced Christian, who has gone out into God, who has felt the thrill of His Spirit, who has dared to believe that the Son of God lives by the Spirit in his life today, just as He lived in the lives of the early Christians, had found the same pregnant power of God in himself and upon laying his hands in faith upon others who are sick, has seen with his own eyes the healing of the sick take place, and realized the transmission of Divine Virtue. And today millions of men and women trust God only for the healing of their body from every character and form of disease.

What, then, is this means of healing that Jesus gave as a divine gift to Christianity forever? It is the living HOLY Spirit of God, ministered by Jesus Christ to the Christian soul transmitted by the Christian because of his faith in the word of Jesus, through his soul and his hands to the one who is sick. Thus revealing the law of contact in the mind of Jesus when He gave the commandment: They shall lay their hands on the sick and they SHALL recover. (Mark 16:18)

With praise to God we record to His glory that through twenty-five years in this ministry we have seen hundreds of thousands of persons healed in all parts of the world. They were healed by the power of God. Throughout twenty-five years we have established churches and societies composed of

John G. Lake in Spokane

Christian men and women who had no remedy other than one divine remedy. The Lord Jesus Christ, His redemption and the power of the Spirit of Christ to conquer sin and sickness in the lives of men forever.

In our own city, for years, no day has passed which we have not seen the healing of many. For years we have ministered with our associate pastors in the Church at Spokane alone, to an average of one hundred six per day that come from all quarters of the land, and even some foreign countries, They receive the healing power of God. These healings have included almost every known form of disease.

The majority of these healings have been on persons pronounced hopeless by their physicians, some of them having spent it all, some tens of thousands of dollars, for doctors, medicines and operations and having failed to get the healing they desired. They are turning to God, they find the Lord Jesus Christ and the ministry of healing and the power of God just as efficacious today as it was, thereby demonstrating the truth of the Word of God.

Rev. John G. Lake
340 Rookery Bldg.
Spokane, Wash.

(The final few pages of this article included illegible words and sentence fragments in the original. Any subsequent differences should be minor and not change the message or intent of Dr. Lake.)

Fire of God

The Spokesman-Review, Spokane, WA
Friday June 24, 1921

BUY HOME FOR CHURCH

The Reverend J.G. Lake Reports Purchase on East Riverton

The first general conference of the International Apostolic congress will start next Monday in the Church at Spokane and be in session for a week. One of the chief matters to come up at the business session will be a change in the incorporation papers to provide for an educational department, with schools, colleges and a university.

The Rev. John G. Lake, overseer, yesterday announced the purchase by the church of five acres and a large 14 room house on East Riverton avenue, on the north bank of the Spokane River, two blocks above the Mission avenue bridge, for a reported consideration of $16,000. The educational work of the church, the healing rooms and homes for the ministers will be there.

Two bishops and a number of ministers will be ordained during the conference, which will embrace the churches of the Inland Empire and the work established by Dr. Lake at Portland. The Church at Portland opened a year ago and last Sunday night a congregation of 3900 attended the services in the municipal auditorium at Portland, Dr. Lake reported yesterday.

John G. Lake in Spokane

The Spokesman-Review, Spokane, WA
June 30, 1921

ORGANIZE APOSTOLIC BOARD

The Rev. J.G. Lake and Two Bishops to Control All Church Property.

  The International Apostolic congress, holding its first annual conference here, voted yesterday that the local board for the general conference, incorporated under the laws of this state, should hold all church property throughout the world in trust for the church. For the time being the Church at Spokane acts as the head for the world work.
  The apostolic board is composed of the Rev. John G. Lake, now apostle, and the Rev. D. N. McInturff of this city and the Rev. H. S. Wallace of San Francisco, who will be ordained as bishops here Sunday. The Rev. Mr. Wallace arrives today and will speak tonight.
  To this apostolic board all questions concerning the general church will be referred. One of the first to be referred to the Rev. Mr. Wallace who is to be ordained as missionary bishop to Africa, with charge of African churches in America, is the application of a colored man in the south, who has 140 churches lined up, according to the Rev. Mr. McInturff yesterday.
  The conference yesterday gave its attention to several articles for the new constitution, defining the duties of officers and the status of women. "In Jesus Christ there is no sex, therefore woman is man's equal in the church and shall be admitted to all the offices and privileges on an equal footing with man," is a statement defining woman's status.

The Spokesman-Review, Spokane, WA
Friday July 1, 1921

REVISE CHURCH TRIAL METHOD

Church at Spokane Discusses Procedure Changes

In establishing further rules for the government of their church, ministers of the Apostolic faith in their first annual conference in The Church at Spokane, the Rev. John G. Lake, apostle, voted yesterday that no bishops should be permitted under any circumstances to listen to complaint from any person against a minister of the church except in the presence of two or more witnesses.

How to try a minister in case he violated the church law was subject for considerable discussion yesterday, the decision being that charges should be proffered by ministers or elders to the diocesan board, including the bishop and two others in the diocese, they to sit upon his case and investigate it. If they think it grave and serious they may suspend him from all ministerial functions until the next annual conference.

The conference heard a resolution offered declaring its stand on the question of divine healing. The resolution will be adopted today, without a doubt, it is said. In effect, the resolution follows: "While the world recognizes doctors, physicians, mental healing and other systems of healing of disease, we offer to the world the very best, namely, healing by prayer."

The Rev. Mr. Wallace, who comes here to be ordained as bishop to Africa, will discuss the labor question tomorrow night with a special sermon to men. He also speaks tonight.

Newspaper ads and announcements from Lake's time in Spokane

DIVINE HEALING DEPARTMENT

Lake's Divine Healing Institute

340 Rookery Bldg.   Phone Main 1463

The Local Church Services are as Follows at the
Knights of Pythias Castle
Cor. Riverside and Jefferson Sts.

SUNDAY SERVICES—Preaching 11 a. m. Special Divine Healing. Teaching and Demonstration Service at 3 p. m.

HEALING ROOM SERVICES—346 Rookery building.

SUNDAY NIGHT—8 o'clock, for Prayer and Testimony.

REV. HALFORD'S LECTURE—Wednesday Evening, 8 p. m.

REV. LAKE'S LECTURE—Friday evening, 8 o'clock.

SPECIAL DIVINE HEALING MEETING—Thursday, 2:30 p. m. At close of service the sick are prayed for.

THE HEALING ROOMS are open every week-day from 10 a. m. until 4 p. m. Private interview with prayer and laying on of hands is given each one desiring ministry.

REV. JOHN G. LAKE
Overseer and Founder of Divine Healing Institute of Spokane

The Church at Spokane

JOHN G. LAKE, Overseer

1387

Personal Interviews With Prayer and Laying on of Hands in the Past Week

THE MAILS HAVE ALSO BROUGHT MANY STORIES OF WONDERFUL HEALINGS THROUGH PRAYER FOR THE ABSENT.

Masonic Temple
Services

Sunday, 11 a. m., communion of the Lord's supper. Every lover of our Lord Jesus Christ is invited to partake.

Sunday, 3 p. m., special address by the Rev. Mr. Lake. Subject-text, "For the gifts and callings of God are without repentance."

Healing Rooms
340 Rookery Building

Tel. Main 1463.
Open every week day from 10 to 4.

DIVINE HEALING DEPARTMENT

Lake's Divine Healing Institute

340 Rookery Bldg. Phone Main 1463

The Local Church Services are as Follows at the Masonic Temple:

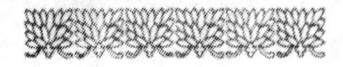

SUNDAY SERVICES—Preaching 11 a. m. Special Divine Healing, Teaching and Demonstration Service at 3 p. m.

HEALING ROOM SERVICES—340 Rookery building.

SUNDAY NIGHT—8 o'clock, for Prayer and Testimony.

REV. OSBORNE'S LECTURE—Wednesday Evening, 8 p. m.

REV. LAKE'S LECTURE—Friday evening, 8 o'clock.

SPECIAL DIVINE HEALING MEETING—Thursday, 2:30 p. m. At close of service the sick are prayed for.

THE HEALING ROOMS are open every week-day from 10 a. m. until 4 p. m. Private interview with prayer and laying on of hands is given each one desiring ministry.

REV. JOHN G. LAKE
Overseer and Founder of Divine Healing Institute of Spokane.

Zion Apostolic Church

John G. Lake, Overseer

Our lists show that surgeons, doctors of medicine, professional nurses, practitioners, mental healers and psychological instructors all come to our healing rooms, and the

Lord Heals Them

And the simple way of the

Cross of Christ

is the true and powerful way of healing for spirit, soul and body.

Sunday services at Knights of Pythias Castle at 11 a. m. and 8 p. m. Healing Rooms 340 Rookery Bldg. Tel. Main 1463.

The Church at Spokane

JOHN G. LAKE, Overseer

*Where People Are Saved
From Sin and Healed
of Diseases
Every Day of the Year*

Services at **MASONIC TEMPLE** SUNDAYS ONLY
11 A.M.—3 P.M.

*Personal Ministration
at Healing Rooms Every Day
10 to 4 Through Prayer
and Laying on of Hands*

THE CHURCH AT SPOKANE

JOHN G. LAKE, Overseer

WHY do 200 persons come to our healing rooms for ministry every day?

Why do we have the largest attendance at our weekly meetings of any church in the city?

Why is it necessary to have public baptism services of large numbers each week?

Answer—the spirit and power of God is working in our midst to save and heal.

SUNDAY SERVICES

At Knights of Pythias Temple

Corner Riverside and Jefferson

11 a.m. and 3 p.m.

Healing Rooms, 340 Rookery Bldg.
Phone Main 1463

The Church at Spokane

JOHN G. LAKE, Overseer

See the Sunday Spokesman-Review for Our Contribution to the Religious Life of the Inland Empire

A FULL PAGE
ENTIRE CHURCH SERVICE

We are trying to demonstrate what the real Christian church should be and accomplish.

OUR HEALING ROOMS
at 340 Rookery Bldg., Spokane

are open from 10 a. m. to 9 p. m. every day for personal ministry through prayer and laying on of hands for healing or the reception of the holy spirit for your peculiar need. Our telephone is Main 1463. We are ministering to hundreds of influenza cases and not one of them has died. Jesus is the healer still.

The Church at Spokane
John G. Lake, Overseer
DIVINE HEALING

The prayer of faith, with the laying on of hands, is God's prescription for healing, and according to our faith so shall the result be.

I prophesy a day to come when divine healing will be recognized throughout the world as the highest and surest system of healing practice known to man. It will be known to be both spiritual and scientific. We need to recognize a new science, and one day our schools will teach the science of pneumatology — the science of spirit.

Public Services
at
Knights of Pythias Castle

Sunday at 11 a. m. and 3 p. m.

Healing Rooms at 340 Rookery Building, open every day for personal ministration.

Phone Main 1463.

Lake with Cyrus B. Fockler

The Church at Spokane
Sunday at 3 P. M.

100 Witnesses

will testify of their personal healing at the Masonic Temple service. Preachers, doctors and doubters are especially invited.

JOHN G. LAKE, Overseer.

THE NEWEST TRUEST NEWS

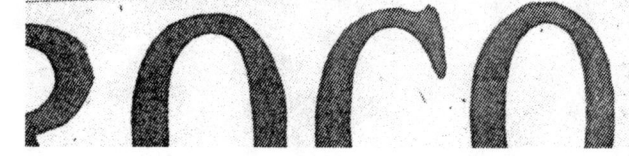

ZION APOSTOLIC CHURCH

John G. Lake, Overseer

Divine Healing as the Greatest Presbyterian Author Sees It, Expressed in a Personal Letter to the Rev. Lake

"Religion in its essence and at its best is but an attitude. It is the attitude that 'The Spirit of Life' in Christ is the Spirit of Life that is groaning and trembling to find expression in every one of us. As our faith is in the indwelling, outworking power of the Father in us, so shall the life of liberty and victory be in each of us. If that life is not for as complete a victory in you and me, and in all, as it was in Jesus, it is nothing.

"Faith is the faculty for accepting this as our heavenly birthright and everlasting inheritance. In this life, sin and sickness and death are done with, and will not have dominion over us. In this faith we have received the preventive medicine for the soul-sick and body-sick and death-struck race, for our complete deliverance. This is the faith that is 'the victory that overcomes the world.'"—Frank N. Riale, Secretary Presbyterian Board of Education, New York City. Author of "The Sinless, Sickless, Deathless Life."

Sunday Services at Knights of Pythias Castle at 11 a. m. and 2 p. m. Healing Rooms 240 Rookery Bldg. Tel. Main 1463.

The Zion Apostolic Church

JOHN G. LAKE, *Overseer*

Sunday Services Knights of Pythias Castle.
Cor. Riverside and Jefferson.

11 a. m. address by

Herman J. Benton, M.D.

3 p. m. address by

Rev. John G. Lake

Subject, the

"Everlasting Gospel".

Healing Rooms 340 Rookery Bldg

Open for ministry every week day.   Phone Main 1463.

The Church at Spokane

John G. Lake, Overseer

OUR HEALING ROOMS

at 340 Rookery Building

ARE OPEN FOR PRIVATE INTERVIEWS AND MINISTRATION through prayer and laying on of hands, from 10 a. m. till 9 p. m. every day during the epidemic; Sunday also. Phone Main 1463.

The Church of Spokane

Christian Doubters Are Invited to Attend

Rev. Lake's 3 P. M. Service at the Masonic Temple Sunday

If you do not want to be convinced, stay away.

HEALING ROOM
PHONE MAIN 1463

THE CHURCH AT SPOKANE

John G. Lake, Overseer.

Explorations in the Soul Country

A Series of Sunday Afternoon Addresses at the

MASONIC TEMPLE
3 P. M.

HEALING ROOMS
Rookery Bldg., open every week day.
Telephone Main 1463.

The 1924 Healing Revival in Spokane

The 1924 Healing Revival

This chapter is a compilation of articles from 1924 which covered the tent meetings held by John G. Lake during the summer as well as a personal letter from Rev. Lake forwarded to the faithful from the church in Portland.

The newspaper made it a point to send as many of its reporters to Lake's healing tents as was possible. This will explain the different tones you may pick up in each article. I felt that it was important to include those articles in favor of the ministry that was going on as well as the opposed in order to make a clearer picture for the reader. As Lake once said, "All of our cards are on the table."

It is this sentiment that makes it important that the story of the "pretty little deaf girl," who could actually hear, be included. It is important that an article was included about a meeting where no healings were seen to have taken place. To only include the favorable articles or news of John G. Lake's ministry would weaken the testimony of faithfulness and anointing that he invested his life to bring us. The God we serve doesn't need to be apologized for. I pray that this account of the 1924 Healing Revival in Spokane leaves you encouraged and blessed.

John G. Lake in Spokane

Thursday, July 3, 1924 The Spokane Press

MODERN MIRACLES

Spokane minister announces he will cure by faith and invites physicians to check up on his promised performances.

Are the days of miracles past? Can prayer make the blind see? The lame walk? The deaf hear?

Can John G. Lake, one time millionaire, who will open a series of evangelistic meetings in Spokane next Sunday evening, prove to Spokane that disease can be overcome by the "prayer of faith?"

Is Lake right in his declaration that "the power of God is just the same today," or did he give up his $50,000 a year job with a nationally known insurance company to follow an illusion?

Lake, who is the head of the "Church Elect" in Spokane and who has a chain of forty churches and missions in the United States and Canada, makes the most startling claims of any of the nationally known "healing evangelists." He never asks an applicant for healing if he is a sinner or saint, a Protestant or a Catholic, a Jew or Gentile.

"God heals all that have an honest soul and any degree of faith," says Dr. Lake.

"Healing the sick is one of God's ways for preparing the people for His message," is the way Dr. Lake explains this unusual belief. "If a man is healed of his diseases he is fertile ground for God's teachings."

But more startling even than his declaration that "healing is for saint and sinner alike," is Dr. Lake's assertion that he welcomes medical investigation. "Tell the doctors,"

Fire of God

said Lake today, "to bring their incurables and their lecture subjects. Bring the hopeless cases, and those who have been under observation for a long time. We will pray for them, and declare them healed, we will turn them over again to the doctors for examination. I am willing to let this be the test of the truth of the message I bring."

The first meeting of the monthly series starts Sunday night in a tent at Ash and Chelan. At 7:30 there will be a song service. Preaching begins at 8 o'clock. There will be a meeting each night during the rest of July.

With Dr. Lake in his campaign are associated Rev. F.B. Eastmand of North Dakota, Rev. George W. Bailey of the Church of God, Spokane, and Rev. J.N. Clos of Bellingham, Wash.

Other ministers from the Lake string of churches throughout the United States and Canada will be brought to Spokane during the series of meetings.

Healing meetings will be on Thursday nights only.

Today Mr. Lake issued the following invitation:

"Bring your sick, and your well, bring the halt, the lame and the disease ridden, bring the sinner and the saint, the Protestant and the Catholic. God's message is for all. Healing is for all."

John G. Lake in Spokane

Friday, July 4, 1924 The Spokane Press

LAKE CLAIMS HE ENDED EPIDEMIC IN SOUTH AFRICA
Converted General de Wet, Boer leader, who arose against the British.

Who is John G. Lake? The man who claims that thru prayer the sick can be healed, the maimed made whole, and who Sunday night will open a series of meetings in a tent at Chelan and Ash in an effort to prove his claims to Spokane. Lake, head of the "Church Elect" in Spokane, was interviewed by a Press reporter today. The following facts about his career were uncovered.

Since the age of 21 his life has been one of unusual adventure in the far corners of the world.

A graduate of Northwestern University, then manager of agents for a nationally known insurance company. Later the man who outlined the native policy adopted by the Smuts government in South Africa. Then a missionary, who after five years work in South Africa established 125 European churches, and native congregations totaling 5000 members, with 500 native preachers.

Last of all a healer, who takes the Bible as his authority and teaches that not only is God able to save the souls of man, but to heal the bodies and keep them well.

Lake is the man who was voted the thanks of the Transvaal Parliament because of his labors during the fever epidemic in the M'Shanagaan and Basuto country in the Zultspansberg District in 1910, when the fever killed more than 25 percent of the entire native and white population in that country.

Fire of God

Reported to Botha

Without any means of curing the fever except prayer, Lake with a party of missionaries invaded the disease ridden country and worked among the natives. His was the first report of the plague situation to be received by General Louis Botha, Premier of South Africa, who immediately placed Lake in charge of the situation until 50 ox wagon loads of supplies and a few government officials could arrive from Pretoria.

"Because of our faith," said Lake today, "We escaped the fever so deadly to the white man, and prayed and worked among those stricken by the plague, praying for thousands and seeing thousands healed. It was the demonstration of the power of God that converted General Hans de Wet, Boer leader who rebelled at the beginning of the late war, to our teachings."

Came here ten years ago

In 1914, Lake came to Spokane to establish headquarters for the string of Lake missions in America. Because of dissension in the local church, Lake moved the headquarters of his work to Portland, but is now in Spokane to re-establish headquarters here.

"The same God that healed the natives of their fever in South Africa will heal the sick of Spokane," said Lake today. "Our meetings during July are for the purpose of proving this to all."

John G. Lake in Spokane

Saturday July 5, 1924 The Spokane Press

100, HEALED BY FAITH, TO TELL ABOUT MIRACLES

Lake arranging testimony meeting as part of services here.

"Cured maniacs will tell how they were healed by Divine power, during the Rev. John G. Lake's healing revival that starts Sunday night," Dr. Lake declared Saturday. Former drunkards, morphine fiends, opium eaters, cripples and cancer victims will testify to the healing power of faith.

"More than 100 individuals, most of them Spokane residents, will recite their miracles," he declared.

"More than 100 miracles of Divine healing will be presented at the testimony meeting, which will take until about the middle of July," said Lake. "Most of these cases are well known to local doctors, and the fact that they have been healed cannot be disputed, because their friends, and neighbors, who can be reached at any time, have seen them both before and after their healings."

"Our object is to demonstrate the power of God. Our hope is that once the people of this city are convinced that healings do take place, and that they are the work of God, and not of man, that many souls will turn from their sins, and find peace and happiness in the Lord."

According to Lake every testimony will be substantiated by persons who knew the one healed both before and after the healing. "We will present no testimony which can not be substantiated either by the family physician, or by reliable witnesses," said Lake today. "We want to so impress the people of Spokane with the truth of our message that when this series of meetings is over, there can be no doubt left in the minds of the citizens."

The first meeting of the July series of healing, teaching, and testimony meetings starts Sunday night at 7:30. The tent in which the meetings will be held nightly during July is situated at the corner of Chelan and Ash. Hollywood, Northwest Boulevard and Cleveland streetcars go within a block or two of the canvas tabernacle. Preaching starts nightly at 8 o'clock. The half hour between 7:30 and 8 will be devoted to the singing of Gospel songs and testimonies.

John G. Lake in Spokane

Monday July 7, 1924 The Spokane Press

ADVENTURES IN RELIGION
Lake opens evangelist campaign. 150 claim they are healed. Old-fashioned Gospel Meeting. Working girl tells of cure.

by John Dewitt

Occupying six or more big lots on the corner of Chelan and Ash streets you will find the three big tents of the Rev. John G. Lake. There were plenty of good seats last evening when he opened his evangelistic campaign aided by a number of his ministers, a fine large choir, a splendid trio of two violins and piano and organ and a well-known blind singer, Clarence Carlille, who sang with that sweet voice of his, "Nothing Between." It was a real old fashioned camp meeting along salvation lines with little sermons by the Rev. Eastman, Rev. Clos, and Rev. Lake.

A large number of people came to the penitent form seeking Christ as their Saviour.

When Mr. Lake asked for uplifted hands from those who had been healed definitely by prayer we counted exactly 150 people. Then he called for individual testimony on healing. Lake: "Here is John Woods, whom we call Charley, he lives at Sharp and Nettleton streets and had ulcers in his stomach for 20 years which the doctors could not cure. He was healed by prayer. I am going to let Charley tell you his story. There are a good many people who have an ulcer on their soul that needs healing. Come here Charley, and tell them about your healing."

Fire of God

Tells of healing:

Woods: "For years I suffered agony with ulcers on my stomach and had some of the best doctors, who finally told me they must operate. I heard through a friend how the Rev. Lake had prayed with an old lady at Pullman, Wash., whom the doctors had given up, and she was healed. So I said to myself, I'll go to Lake at the Rookery Bldg., Spokane. When I got downtown I suffered so much pain that I got off on the wrong street, Sprague and Howard, and started up the back stairs instead of the elevator. There were three flights to go and when I got up to the second I suffered so much that I sat down and wondered if I would reach the top. When I arrived in the healing rooms I met Mrs. Meero, the lady in charge of the rooms. She said Mr. Lake was out but that they could help me as God did all the healing. Rev. Halford and Mrs. Meero then prayed for me and after several minutes Halford said, 'Has it gone?' I said, 'No, and I don't expect it to go in seven minutes.' Then they prayed with me three minutes more and I was instantly healed. I had not been able to eat right for several years and the minute I got healed I wanted a beef steak so I went to a butcher and bought five pounds and took it home, walked in and told my wife to cook it. She thought I was crazy and said, 'John, what's the matter, are you sick?' ' No,' I said, 'Thank God, I am well' and ate the whole of it and it tasted mighty good, too."

Lake: "You see how it is, the Lord is not dead after all. Where is your faith? Stand up, Mrs. Boyles. This lady lives at the Gandy Hotel on Sprague near Monroe. When she was four years of age living at Lewiston, Idaho, she was made a cripple hunchback. She remained that way until 44 years of age, when she was healed by prayer through us and became 6 ½ inches taller the minute her back was healed. Then her right leg which hung and dangled and had nothing for a foot but a mass of flesh, finally began to grow right, her toes came out of the little mass

John G. Lake in Spokane

of flesh and the baby ribs began to grow, and now she has a foot all right. Her hip was nothing but a mass of muscle and that is now beginning to grow along all right. You have never heard of a record of a case like this which the physicians have cured, but praise God. God can do it every time."

Working Girl Cured

"Come here, Louise. This is Louise Hengle, a working girl, 20 years of age. At eight years of age this girl got locked shoulders from rheumatism and was hunched all up and could not lift her arms. At 5 o'clock today we prayed for her and she was instantly healed. Look at her shoulders now. Raise your arms, Louise. (Louise did so, straight above her head) You see the best things come from heaven."

"Come here, Grover. This is Grover Risdon, who lives at W1520 Clarke Avenue. How old are you Grover?"
"I am eleven years old."   "Do you go to school?"
"Yes, sir; to one of the grade schools and I am in the B grade."
"This boy was born with a closed head so that the top went up and the sides protruded. He could not speak, was paralyzed, was an imbecile and the saliva ran from his mouth and he was that way until four years old. Then his mother, who is here, brought him to us. We prayed for him, God healed him, and you see him today, a splendid, bright boy, doing well in school. There is nothing too hard for God!"

God Does Not Send Sickness

"The old belief that God sent sickness is all nonsense. Here's an illustration." A Sunday School teacher said to the class of ten boys, "Now ,Willie, what have you to be thankful for, what has God done for you?" "Lots," said Willie, "I can run and play and beat all the boys at swimming." Then the teacher turned to a hunchback cripple and said, "Charlie, what has God done for you?" Charlie looked up with a sad expression and said, "He nearly finished me."

"Come here, Mrs. Eastman - - this is Mrs. Tom Eastman, who lives at Sharon. She has had twenty-six major operations, then was sent to Los Angeles, where the doctors used her for four years as an 'awful example,' being their experimental subject. She also became a dope fiend. Her father who is a rich farmer, lost several farms, a number of good houses and finally 400 cords of wood in paying doctor bills, until he was broke. She finally came to us and Mrs Lake and myself prayed with her and she was instantly healed of her tuberculosis and later of the dope. She said that a hand seemed to reach down into her vitals and a voice said, 'you are healed,' and she was from that minute. She is now happily married and living near us. You see that God is not dead, for the Lord Jesus Christ is the same yesterday, today, and tomorrow. The wonderful Lover, Saviour, and Healer of mankind."

John G. Lake in Spokane

Monday, July 7, 1924
Editorial in the Spokane Press

Dear Press: Your article regarding Rev. John G. Lake in the issue of July 3rd is to me most interesting. I have known John G. Lake for 30 years. I first met him in Chicago when he was a Methodist preacher. Later he was in the insurance business in Chicago, with a big company. At this time I was his guest on his cattle and sheep ranch, 150 miles from Custer, S.D. We hunted coyotes together and slept in a sheep wagon for six weeks.

Lake would pray for every sick cowboy and would ride incredible distances to a sick woman or child, and I can assure you I saw many wonderful healings through him.

Some years later I went to South Africa and met him there in his great work. Lake was held in high esteem by Cecil John Rhodes, Jan Smuts, ex-premier of South Africa, Louis Botha and others of the statesmen of South Africa, where for a number of years he was a national figure. In 1911 I met him by appointment in the Belgian Congo. He was then on an exploring expedition in the interests of his great South African mission.

Lake impressed me as the most selfless man I have ever known. On one occasion Cecil John Rhodes said to me: "I have never taken much stock in religion, but as you watch Lake and see his faith in God, his love for humanity and his seeming answers to prayer it makes one believe the stories of the Bible are all right."

Lake is a native-born faith creator. The part he played in the reconstruction of South Africa after the shattering of the Boer war made him one of the most loved men in the country, while to the native people he soon became almost an object of worship.   Dr. John J. Oremus

Fire of God

Tuesday, July 8, 1924 The Spokane Press

DR. LAKE WILL TRY HEALING ON THURSDAY NIGHT

"Few ministers expect to have prayers answered," says Rev. J.N. Clos. More than 400 of Spokane's sick and diseased are expected to be on hand for prayer at next Thursday's "healing" meeting to be held in the Church Elect tents at Ash and Chelan, according to Dr. John G. Lake, head of the Lake missions throughout the United States and Canada.

"We have designated Thursday of each week as healing meetings," said Mr. Lake today. "We invite the sick of Spokane and the Inland Empire to be present on those evenings."

30 Testify to Healing

Since the meeting started last Sunday night about 30 have testified that they have been healed of their diseases, despite the fact that the meetings thus far have been teaching meetings, and not healing meetings.

A crowd that almost filled one of the large tents heard the Rev. J.N. Clos, one of Dr. Lake's assistants, speak on "how to pray" at Monday night's meeting.

"Not one minister in 50 prays with any expectation of getting an answer," said Clos. "Can you imagine anything more foolish than continued prayer without any hope of an answer?"

Trouble Not With God

"If you were to speak to me time after time and I should refuse to answer you, how long would you continue your useless talking? Would you not try to find out what the trouble was? Of course you would."

"Well depend on it, when you pray and do not get an answer, the trouble is with you, not with God. He has promised to answer prayer, and He will if you have the least particle of faith."

"Do not forget to return thanks for what God gives you. Prayer is one wing of an eagle— thanks is the other. There will be little flying unless both wings are used." Tuesday night's meeting will be one of teaching and testimony, preparation for the huge healing meeting on Thursday night.

Fire of God

Thursday July 10, 1924 The Spokane Press

DIVINE HEALER ASKS DOCTORS' INVESTIGATION

Lake promises demonstrations of Faith healing at meeting tonight.

Does God still heal the sick?

Tonight this question will be answered for many Spokane persons, if the claims of Dr. John G. Lake head of the Church Elect, who is holding a series of divine healing and teaching meetings in a group of tents at Ash and Chelan, are true.

At 8 p.m. the first healing meeting of the series will start. All the sick of Spokane have been invited to attend and be prayed for according to Lake.

Invites Doctors Too

"I have issued a special invitation to the doctors of the city and have given them permission to examine each applicant for healing, before and after we pray for them," said Lake today. "We have reserved a row of seats for those wishing to investigate the healings."

Plans for the transportation of a large crowd have been completed by the Washington Water Power Company.

"We will be able to handle several thousand persons if necessary," said R.A. Willson, a traffic manager of the W.W.P. Company today. " I will watch closely and if extra cars are needed they will be on hand," he declared. Cleveland, Northwest Boulevard and Hollywood cars go to the Divine healing tents.

John G. Lake in Spokane

Can't Estimate Crowd

"There is no way of estimating in advance the size of the crowd," said Lake this morning. " We have seating capacity for 100, but should a larger crowd than this be on hand we will roll up the flaps of the tents and those who come late will be able to stand in the open and hear and see distinctly."

Dr. Lake will have charge of tonight's meeting. He will be the speaker tonight for the first time since the meetings opened last Sunday.

Fire of God

Friday July 11, 1924 The Spokane Press

CROWDS HEAR TALES OF MIRACLE CURE IN LAKE'S GOSPEL TENT

Preacher insists days of heavenly acts against illness are not past; Many ask prayers to end ailments.
By John Dewitt

The Rev. John Lake and his band of evangelists had his big tents packed with a curious and attentive audience last evening, many of whom had come long distances to hear and to see what was going on.

Automobiles were lined up on the nearby streets. There were two or three hundred people lined up on the outside of the tent who could not get in and find seats.

Lake spoke of his work in Spokane, how he had come here years ago, the courtesy he had received from the Rev. Mr. Grier who had opened his church for him and told him to go ahead and preach the way he liked.

Twenty Ministers

After six months he had started the work of his own and it had grown to a vast proportion. At that time he had gone to Portland, he had 20 ministers on his staff in Spokane alone, besides a large number on the outside. Correspondence all over the world, several hundred people being prayed for every day and an immense lot of healings that were a blessing not only to the community but to the world at large.

Lake took up his New Testament, read some verses and commented upon them as he went along. He showed the work of Jesus in healing in the old days and said:

"Shall we place healing only in past ages, or do miracles

John G. Lake in Spokane

exist today? I propose to show by people in this tent that miracles do exist today, for about me are some of the worst cases that you have ever seen of cripples and others whom the doctors had long ago given up."

"God alone can heal these, and He has and does. When I worked here before, Spokane was the healthiest city in the United States, according to governmental records. Is it today?" Lake now turned to his audience and called up several people who had been marvelously healed, under the administration of himself and his assistants and asked the audience what they thought about it. Said he:

"Here are real demonstrations of the power of God to work miracles today upon the bodies and souls of men and women. You people want proofs. Here they are."

Then he called for the people to come up and be prayed for, and so many of them came that soon he and his assistants were busy and people were waiting to be treated.

Robert Clark, W. 1520 Clark, was an asthmatic for years and was an experimental subject used by doctors at San Francisco. Nothing availed him. He came back here in a dying state and was healed.

Lake- - "How long did your healing take?"

Clark- - "It was instant."

Lake- - "Where was it?"

Clark- - "In a hall above the Raad Bros. Store, corner of Main and Wall."

Lake- - "What was it like?"

Clark- - "Something like an electric shock went through me and I knew I was instantly healed."

Lake- - "You see the Spirit of God is a tangible subject. What's the matter with you people? Some of you want pale pills for pink people, and some pink pills for pale people. You have them on your shelves and in your pockets and when you leave home you carry them with you for you seem to be afraid to get away from them. What's the matter with trusting God for a while?"

Another "exhibit" was Grover Risdon, son of Orange A. Risdon, night engineer at the Davenport. He was born with a deformed head, imbecilic, dumb and paralyzed on the right side. Surgeons gave him up, the mother who took the platform with the boy, testified.

Then Began to Talk

"When he was 4 ½ years old he was taken to Lake, at the second administration his paralyzed foot straightened a little and soon afterward began to talk, as a baby does, although he didn't understand the meaning of the words," his mother said. "In seven weeks his skull softened, his head shaped itself permanently and when it hardened again the boy had a symmetrical perfectly shaped skull. He is now in public school."

Among the people prayed for and with was the boy of Mrs. J.F. Lilienthal, W1137 Providence. This boy was a splendid bright little fellow, going to school, when another boy hit him with a hammer on the head and from that minute he has been as far as the doctors are concerned, a hopeless imbecile. Others prayed for:

Little Alice, the daughter of Mrs. Goldie Mace of Deer Park, WA. Child has a large tumor on the throat. Leslie Wooley, young man of epileptic fits, came from Portland, OR. Bert Goodwin, W. 27 Second; cataract. Mrs. A. J. Davidson, insanity, is staying with a friend at 321 Diamond Ave. Hillyard. Mrs. Cora Chase, N272 Ash, paralyzed. Paul Weber, tuberculosis; N222 ½ Division. Nellie Fisher, tuberculosis of the hip and spine, S. 521 Stevens, came here from Portland, OR.

John G. Lake in Spokane

Tuesday July 15, 1924 The Spokane Press
letter to the editor

INSTANTANEOUS CURE

Dear Press: I was greatly pleased to note the publicity your splendid paper is giving to the divine healing tent campaign of Rev. John G. Lake.

I was a practicing attorney in Chicago and became an invalid. The best medical skill failed to relieve me. I was persuaded to see Rev. John G. Lake for his help and healing. I visited him at Indianapolis, Ind. He taught me to look to God direct and to believe he would heal me. Two days later he prayed with me laying his hands on me in prayer. Currents of Divine Spirit coursed through my person from my head to my feet.

In an instant this divine current centered in the diseased portion of my body. A strange tingling sensation, similar to a sleeping foot or hand, pervaded the affected parts and I was perfectly whole in a few minutes.

Later, I became a rheumatic cripple. Rev. Lake had then gone to England. I cabled him that I was coming to him; when I arrived he was just taking ship for Africa. He took me to his cabin and prayed as I never heard any one else pray, with power and unction. This time I was gradually healed from the time of prayer onward for 10 days. Since that time I have been perfectly well.

Arnott W. Stubblefield

Tuesday, July 15, 1924 The Spokane Press

THE PRAYER OF FAITH DOES HEAL THE SICK!

Lake again invites doctors to examine those pronounced cured by praying.

"The prayer of faith does heal the sick."

That is the emphatic statement of Dr. John G. Lake, head of the Church Elect, who is conducting a series of divine healing and revival meetings in a group of tents at Ash and Chelan.

As proof of his startling assertion Lake offers names of persons who have pronounced themselves cured: Mrs. A.C. Carver, wife of the Willys Knight agent at Coeur d' Alene, healed of cancer; Mrs. G.A. Acres, Ford, Idaho, healed of internal disorders and acute indigestion; Mrs. Hattie Neilson W224 ½ Main, healed of a tumor; Mrs. R.H. Hudson, Insley Apartments, healed of cancer.

In addition to those enumerated, Mrs. A. J. Davidson, 321 Diamond Street, Hillyard, invalid for two and one half years after an operation has shown a decided improvement, according to testimony of her nurse. Mrs. Davidson was unable to speak a single word with the exception of "no" until Friday morning. "Now," said her nurse today, "She is beginning to coordinate words and sentences."

"I am offering these particular cases," said Lake, "because each can be checked up on by those wishing to investigate. All are well known cases among local medical men, and each is willing to give all necessary information to those investigating."

John G. Lake in Spokane

"Again, I invite the doctors and other interested persons of Spokane to investigate these healings. We are holding nothing back. Our cards are all on the table. Many doctors were in attendance at last Thursday's meeting. They saw the crippled, the blind and the diseased file past for prayer. They saw the largest array of unfortunates ever assembled in one group in the city of Spokane."

Let Doctors Examine
"Now we are offering them the privilege of examining those prayed for at that time. It is only right that they should take advantage of our invitation. If we are teaching the truth the world should know. Yes, we do more than invite investigation, we demand it."

"I want every single one of those prayed for last Thursday night to be on hand next Thursday evening to tell the results of our prayers. Those who were entirely healed, those who were partially healed, and those who received no healing. I want them to tell frankly and fully just exactly what the results of the prayers were."

Because of the large number of applicants for healing who have announced their wish to receive prayer, it has been necessary for Lake to arrange to hold two healing meetings a week in the future.

Tuesdays and Thursdays will be devoted to healing during the rest of July. The balance of each week will be given over to teaching and testimony meetings. Tonight the first of the Tuesday healing meetings will be held. The meetings start at 8 o'clock.

Wednesday, July 16, 1924 The Spokane Press
Letter to the Editor

SCIENCE PLUS BIBLE

Dear Press: Your highly interesting articles on the life and work of Rev. John G. Lake leads me to acknowledge my appreciation for your bringing Lake out of his too long hiding.

I became interested in Lake in 1889 at Newberry, Mich. Lake was then a theological student while I was an avowed skeptic as a professor of sciences. It then seemed impossible to me to believe the Bible. I thought the statements of Moses were ridiculous and miracles of Jesus a myth.

Lake was a brilliant student. His scientific mind soon marked him as a leader in chemistry and electricity. It was his discovery of natural law in the spiritual world that impelled him to search into the secrets of the nature of God and man and discover the harmonies of that relationship.

John G. Lake comes before the Spokane public with a treasure of spiritual, scientific and experimental knowledge of God beyond that of any other man it has ever been my privilege to know, and my many years of acquaintance with him leads me to believe that Lake is one of the master mystic minds of the age.

A.A. BETTES, Harrison, Idaho.

P.S.— I was the builder of the electric railroad between Spokane and Coeur d' Alene

John G. Lake in Spokane

Wednesday July 16, 1924 The Spokane Press

"PRAISE GOD I CAN WALK"

Shrill screams follow girls cry at Lake healing tent; another woman loses consciousness under stress of violent prayer; Grandma says girl made to hear wasn't deaf.

"Oh, praise God, I can walk!"
Sharp screams followed the cry, screams from a hundred different throats. Two hundred hands waved frantically in the air. Two hundred feet shuffled nervously on the sawdust ground. Then a hundred voices raised to the hymn of "Praise God For All His Blessings," led by Dr. John G. Lake, in his tent on Ash and Chelan.

Janette Estot, colored, 30 had been healed. Healed after an illness of 14 years. Month after month she had suffered with acute indigestion and sciatic rheumatism, they said.

Entered A Cripple

Tuesday evening she had entered the tent a cripple- - so they told the reporter. It had taken two friends to lead her to the platform so that the ministers could pray over her, they said. And sharp pains kept shooting through her body.

Then four ministers gathered about the woman and placing their hands on her, prayed, prayed that the spirit of the devil leave her body, and they said it did.

A few minutes of excited prayer- - the audience joining in. Then the prayers ceased. Dead-like silence crept over the big tent. Tense moments those were. Everyone was waiting to see the miracle God had performed -- for they believe that God still heals the sick.

Fire of God

Then a sharp cry! The signs of suffering left Janette's face. She walked from the platform. "I can walk-- Praise God!" she cried, "Praise God!"

Audience is Frantic

It was a frantic audience that screamed "Praise God- - bless God- - she can walk -- bless God." And above the wild cries of the audience could be heard Janette's voice as she walked up and down the aisle.

"Praise God -- praise God -- I can walk -- I can walk at last." Then a little old lady limped up to the platform- - her hands were clasped over her chest. She was suffering frightfully, she said. Her face showed that.

But she forced a smile and turned to the audience. "I've been healed five times before," she said. But the pain comes back. The doctors don't know what it is -- but it causes me great suffering. This time God will heal it for good though, praise God."

"Praise God -- bless Him," the audience murmured.

Loses Consciousness

Then the four ministers placed their hands on the little old lady's chest and prayed violently. As they shouted for the devil to leave her body, the audience worked up to a tense state of excitement, prayed with the ministers.

"Be gone, you devil, back to hell where you belong," prayed the four ministers.
"Praise God -- praise God," shouted the people in the crowded tent. A shrill scream rang thru the tent.

The next moment the little old lady was lying on the floor of the tent unconscious. Pushing the crowd back, Apostle Lake picked her limp body up and laid it on a bench. The reporter rushed to the woman's side, but was promptly stopped from interfering.

John G. Lake in Spokane

"Don't, Don't a minister cried, "That is the Spirit of God working. You must not interfere. Praise God -- Praise God."

Pay No Attention to Her
The little old lady continued to lie on the bench unconscious. The meeting went on. Teresa Luther, a pretty little girl with bright blue eyes was next in line. She was stone deaf— so they said.

After a few minutes of violent praying the child cried, "I can hear— I can hear." "Praise God, praise God!" chanted the onlookers. "Yes, I can hear wonderfully now," the pretty girl told the reporter. She was with her grandmother— a sweet looking lady with white hair. "So your granddaughter is healed?" asked the reporter.

But she wasn't deaf
"What?" said the grandmother. "Why she's never been deaf. She can't hear any better now than she ever could. We went for a walk tonight and the child dragged me in here. Before I knew it she was up on the platform. She's never been deaf." Then and there the pretty little girl was taken right home to bed and probably spanked.

Numbers of others flocked to the platform -- many claimed to be cured during the ministers prayer. Many in the audience testified to wonderful miracles performed.

Physicians will testify to them; so they say. Then the meeting was over. The little old lady was still lying on the bench unconscious. They would keep her there all night, they said-- until she came to, at least. And as the crowd left the big tent-- the hundred voices kept chanting, "Praise God- - praise God."

Fire of God

Friday July 18, 1924 The Spokane Press

FAITHFUL FLOCK TO TENTS FOR HEALING AT APOSTLE'S HANDS

Belief in Heavenly miracles cannot but impress even those who doubt the efficacy of Evangelist's prayer.

Thursday was healing night at John Lake's tented hall. The large enclosure at Ash and Chelan was packed to the edges, and the side flaps raised that the outside audience in rows of benches out in the open might see and hear.

Right up to the very feet of John Lake and his co-workers on the raised platform crowded those who had come to hear the message of these "chosen apostles of the Lord." And looking over the vast assembly one could not but be impressed by the great sincerity and faith that brought them there. No sound broke the intense silence of the rapt attentive throng but the occasional whimper of a sleepy child or a moaned "Amen- - praise God!" from some troubled believer.

Communion of Song

Then the woman at the piano began to play and the Rev. J.M. Clos of Bellingham started in a voice of liquid persuasiveness:

"I will cling to the old rugged cross and exchange it some day for a crown." The choir, up in front, joined in, then the audience, and then in the communion of song the meeting began.

A young man from Kellogg had been instantly "cured" of appendicitis. The Rev. Lake called him to the platform. The

John G. Lake in Spokane

fellow murmured something in a testimonial and Mr. Lake explained to the listeners:

"For four days this lad had been in a hospital suffering intense pain. Then he and his mother and father and two of our ministers got together and prayed and the hand of God relieved his misery."

The minister suddenly raised to high pitched vehemence: "Do you know what appendicitis is? My friend, I will tell you then how simple it is for the great power that works through us to cure this terrible malady."

The Lord Never Monkeys

"Appendicitis is the contraction of the mouth of the appendix. It is caused by a chill. And I will tell you, my sisters and brothers, that you could take all the dope in the world and it would not have the power to open that outlet to that appendix. It takes the power of God- - brought about as we bring it by the laying on the hands. Scientists advanced the theory that the appendix was a remnant left over from our monkey stage- - but the Lord never monkeys. This disease and the wonderful cures we have affected thru prayer is the greatest illustration I know for the powerlessness of medicine. The Almighty does the relaxing needed-- thru agency of prayer. I never knew of an instance that was not cured in this way."

The young man from Kellogg slipped away to a bench in front. Mr. Lake announced that the subject for his evening's talk would be "Your inheritance from Jesus Christ," for over an hour- - with a dynamic force that cannot be denied- - he held the audience with stories of his healing ministry and the demons of darkness and disease that he can cast out from the multitudes coming to him for help.

Fire of God

Devil is the Father of Ills

"Through disobedience, sin, disease, and sickness, came into the world," he roared. "Disobedience is the mother of all ills and the devil is the father."

"Have you ever cast out devils? NO? Well bless your old hearts, some day you will wake up and know your power and be a prince instead of a weakly, wibbly, wobbly pauper in the power of God."

The sermon finally concluded. The healing service began. Up to the front came those clamoring to be healed. Supported by parents, friends and groping along, hobbled, limped and shuffled those who sought relief for their infirmities.

One cannot scoff

If one could disregard the great faith and purpose that brought them here and the suffering and agony of mind that craved succor from any means, the healing manifestations by Mr. Lake and his helpers would have seemed ludicrous and irreverent.

But a conscientious observer cannot scoff at such a gathering of misery weakened souls. If that group of sufferers kneeling at the "apostles" feet and submitting to the almost grotesque manipulation from the healers as they commanded the "demons" to depart from the afflicted body, contained one who was cured -- and there were many who professed to be -- then these meeting must be a means to an end.

Mrs. W.J. Stanifer, N4023 Napa, who had been in constant pain for the three weeks from a 10 year abcess in her lungs, claimed to have lost the pain immediately when prayed over.

S.B. Rainey, E824 Tenth, suffering from rheumatism felt he could be cured when he came. He said he was.

John G. Lake in Spokane

Filled With Faith

They brought to Mr. Lake idiots, epileptics, and paralytics. There were no instances last evening of any improvement. But they all seemed to be filled with the faith -- and were sure that miracles would be performed -- in time.

Among those who sought prayer relief were: C.E. Skalton, E1014 Illinois, kidney trouble; N.A. Reneau, N4940 Magnolia, tumor; Alice Mace 13, Deer Park, tumor; Mrs. D.C. Richards, Riverside, cancer; T.H. Allison, E3224 Bridgeport, deafness; Mrs. Ray Murphy, 3721 Princeton, tuberculosis; Charles Ring, Ontario, Canada, ulcers of the stomach.

There were many, many others. Mr. Lake told them he would keep the meetings going until all had a chance to be saved through his administrations. And it was near to midnight when most of the audience left the tent, but there were even those left behind praying for the afflicted.

Fire of God

Saturday July 19, 1924 The Spokane Press

Little Alice Has Such Faith!
Prays for Tumor to Disappear— and She Knows it Will

By Irene Burns

Such faith - in those big blue eyes! Peering out from under a corduroy hat of Alice blue - those big blue eyes. Eyes that immediately attract attention to little Alice's pretty face. Two little feet twitch nervously as they hang from the bench. Two little arms - frail little arms are crossed over her neck. Two little hands are clenched tightly. Swish! Rows of white organdie ruffles rumple as little Alice moves excitedly. Little Alice is sitting in the front row at Dr. John G. Lake's tent on Ash and Chelan again tonight.

Hides Big Tumor

The two frail little arms are trying to hide a great ugly tumor on the little girls neck - a very painful tumor. It is. Alice has had it most of the eight years of her life - and oh -how it hurts!

The two little hands are clutching some pennies - moist pennies those are. Alice has saved them for the collection box. Pennies might not mean much to some people, but to little Alice - her contribution has meant a real sacrifice. Daily she has passed the corner store to look longingly at the tempting display of gum drops, licorice and all-day suckers! But little Alice thinks of the minister - the healer - who is going to take away her tumor so she puts the pennies back in her pocket and walks on.

And that tumor - my it hurts! It hurts so every time Alice swallows. And Alice knows it isn't becoming.

John G. Lake in Spokane

Knows God Will Heal

But little Alice's life has been brighter the last two weeks - she has something to live for now - everything to live for. So the blue eyes are shining brightly tonight. The dreadful pain is almost forgotten. Alice knows that Rev. Lake will take away her tumor.

Night after night she sits patiently in the front row waiting for God to heal her. Night after night they have prayed over Alice - but somehow that soon - maybe tonight - her tumor will go away.

So tonight little Alice's eyes are just a little brighter - a little bluer. Her sad smile is just a little happier - the white organdie ruffles swish a little more than often - for Alice is excited - she is going to be healed.

And those eyes - such faith- in those big blue eyes!

Fire of God

Wed. July 23, 1924 The Spokane Press

MIRACLES FAIL, IMP OF TRAGEDY STALKS IN TENT

Hope grows dim in eyes of many as faith cures are not accomplished. Imps of tragedy stalked Tuesday night in Apostle Lake's "Divine healing" tents at Ash and Chelan. Wrought to a high pitch in expectation of miracles, many were disappointed when miracles did not transpire.

Blind, dumb, deformed, cancerous, scores tottered or limped to the healing platform.

Cries of the devout had preceded them -- "Bless God!" and "Begone you devil!" and "Bless preacher Lake!" For two hours the apostle had preached telling stories, many humorous, of his long healing ministries in North America and South Africa.

Pitiful Procession

Then came the pitiful procession of the crippled and ailing.

Loved ones watched with baited breath for the "miracle man" to heal their children, wives, or friends.

For 30 minutes the tent was filled with the cries of the apostle, his four assistants and the sick souls seeking to be made whole.

Preachers raised their hands high in the air and called on God to kill "the damned thing," that inhabited the twisted bodies.

Spellbound watchers in the audience waited for miracles. So far the unprejudiced observer could see there were none. The parents of one little girl, a victim of the goiter, watched with baited breath while Lake prayed over her. Their

John G. Lake in Spokane

eyes pleaded with more eloquent terms than Lake or any man could ever pray. The little girl turned and came away uncured. The parents' eyes lost their luster. Hope faded from them like the beauty of the golden sunset banishes before the darkness of the night.

Tragedy Seems Victor

With the numerous pitiful little scenes like these enacted on every side the imps of tragedy seemed to be laughing derisively in their victory.

One woman in the choir who was singing during the miracle hour was overcome by a fit of coughing. Her head drooped, her body convulsed, her face turned an ashen gray. The choir kept on singing, the prayers kept on praying and still she coughed.

After the spasm of coughing passed away, she raised her feeble voice in song again and continued singing until the end of service. That woman had faith.

The reporter who was sent there to cover the story came away without a name. The tragedy of it all, left him suspended in a swirl of emotions somewhat the same as those experienced by theatergoers who have just witnessed one of Shakespeare's tragedies.

Fire of God

Thursday, July 24, 1924 The Spokane Press

FAITH HEALER TO ASK SHOW-DOWN FROM MEDICOS

Offers $500 to community chest if committee not sure of cures.

John G. Lake, divine healer, has called for a "showdown," a challenge, to test the truth of divine healing was issued to the medical profession of Spokane by Lake Thursday. Lake demands that a committee of five be appointed to examine 50 applicants for healing. The condition of the patients after 30 days ministrations to be the basis on which the committee makes its report.

Offers $500 To Charity

The challenge follows:

"Because the world is woefully unaware that healing for the body was included in the atonement of Jesus Christ, just as was salvation for the soul, and as I desire to do all in my power to bring this truth to the attention of the people. I hereby issue the following challenge."

"Let a committee consisting of one allopathic physician, one osteopath, one chiropractor, one divine healer, and one layman, to be the choice of Mayor Fleming, be appointed to examine 50 applicants for healing at one of our Thursday night tent meetings. Then let us minister to the patients for 30 days."
"At the end of that time let the patients be re-examined by the committee. If we cannot show cases of perfect healing among the selective number, I will make a gift of $500 to the Spokane Community Chest or to any charitable organization agreed upon by the committee.

John G. Lake in Spokane

Three Claim Healing

Three persons today presented signed statements in which they claimed instantaneous healings in the healing tents at Ash and Chelan.

Mrs. J.B. Forrey, E1915 Eleventh, said: "I was instantly healed Tuesday night, July 22, when John G. Lake and his assistants prayed for me. I was suffering from a form of locomotorataxia, caused by a fall on a polished floor two years ago. I could not walk straight, but would go sideways and stagger. I am so well that I worked all day Wednesday. Oh, it is so good to be well."

Mrs. A. Bearden of Apartment 19, Jay Cox Building, Walla Walla, now staying at E3 Third, declared she was instantly healed of tuberculosis of the hip at Tuesday night's meeting.

"When I was prayed for I was instantly healed and arose and walked," says her letter.

Pronounced Incurable

"I was operated on twice and pronounced an 'incurable' from internal disorders," is the way Mrs. G.B. Stagger, W1927 Broadway, starts her letter. "I was instantly healed at Tuesday night's healing meeting, and relieved of my terrible suffering." "More than half of the cases prayed for showed no evidence of illness," said Lake today. "Many of the troubles of those prayed for are internal, and the only way to let the world know that they have them, is to have a medical certificate."

"That is why I demanded a committee of five. My statement and the statements of the patients alone are not sufficient. Let the doctors make the statements. Then the people of Spokane and the Inland Empire will know." The next healing meeting will be eight tonight.

Fire of God

Friday, July 25, 1924 The Spokane Press

APOSTLE LAKE'S FLOCK BELIEVES FAITH CURES

Many who came to scoff are convinced by testifier's undeniable sincerity.

By Chester G. Reese

The idea seems to be that every reporter on The Press shall attend at least one of Apostle Lake's "divine healing" meetings.

This one felt like scoffing when he boarded the West Cleveland Car for the faith tents of the Church Elect at Ash and Chelan. He felt less like scoffing when he came away.

The atmosphere began to take shape even in the streetcar. The sick, lame, and halt, with canes, crutches and limps soon filled the car. The faces of these people seemed to shine in a peculiar way.

Motorman Rebukes Joke

Even the motorman, accustomed as he is to this environment, every Tuesday and Thursday night, seemed to get into the spirit. He held his head high and handled his vehicle with great surety and care, as if proud to do his bit in the curing of the world's ills.

"Is this the Holy Roller church out on this line?" asked a young man who, like the reporter was inclined to be skeptical.

"No," replied the motorman, so shortly that the young man got tired of his joke and meekly went to the rear of the car. Arrived at the tent, the reporter found the first song in progress and feeling rather self-conscious, slipped into a chair in the rear

John G. Lake in Spokane

of the congregation. But no such luck. He was spotted and dragged up to the platform where he was given a chair.

Felt Rather Foolish

He had never been up in front of a religious congregation before and felt rather foolish. But when he dared look around he forgot his embarrassment in studying the interesting show going on before him.

They were singing "This Is Like Heaven To Me," and their inspired faces showed that they took it literally. Spirits other than those of fermenti were moving these people. They had something genuine. No audience as large as that could have faked religious fervor.

And then the testimonials began. Dozens in that congregation and, under oath to God almighty solemnly swore that the Rev. John G. Lake and his disciples had actually knocked the devil out of them, that the Spirit of the Lord had entered their beings and left them clean and whole.

The Cures They Tell

C. Hollingsworth, E1815 Eighth, had been instantly cured of tuberculosis. None of Mrs. Charles B. LeDoux's five children were brought into the world with the aid of a doctor. Mrs. Emma Johnson, E1312 Thirteenth Avenue, had been given over to the devil, in the form of paralysis, which the doctors admitted they could not cure. Then she "turned to the old fashioned God of our fathers" and He cured her.

With both feet in the grave, Harry Greenfield, W1720 First, He had turned to God, who snatched him from his deathbed, he said. Four of the best doctors in Spokane had given Harry up and had admitted at the time that the cure was a miracle.

Mrs. Thomas Olson, E1103 Providence, had vomited up the devil in the form of a cancer of the stomach when the apostles of God had laid their hands on her.

A thirty pound tumor had not been too heavy for God to lift out of the body of Mrs. E.H. Tiske, N3918 Washington.

These People Believe
There was no denying that these people were speaking the truth as they saw it, and no matter what others may think, they actually believed that faith, and nothing else cured them. Many others testified and 102 hands were raised in response to Lake's request that all those who had been healed signify with the usual sign.

No miracles were performed Thursday night -- much to the relief of the reporter, whose cynicism had been somewhat shaken by the devout testimony.

The whole thing seemed odd, but on analysis, the theory of divine healing was not a new one. It began before Christianity.

John G. Lake in Spokane

Monday, July 28, 1924 The Spokane Press

HEALED BY GOD 200 TELL LAKE

27 say they have believed for over 25 years.

"All those in the tent who have been healed by the power of God rise to your feet."

Immediately more than 200 members of the congregation in the divine healing tents arose when Dr. John G. Lake made this request during the special healing meeting Sunday afternoon.

"To show the skeptical that divine healing is not a temporary affair, I want those who have trusted God for healing for more than 25 years to raise their hands," said Lake. Twenty-seven hands were raised.

"God is not only able to heal you, but keep you well. Many professed Christians pretend to believe in the prayer of faith, but always add the qualification, 'if it be thy will,' Lake said. " It is God's will to heal you, just as it is His will to save you. Don't pray 'if it be Thy will' anymore. Let the testimony of these 200 healed persons convince you that it is always God's will to fulfill his promises."

Fire of God

Tuesday, July 29, 1924 The Spokane Press

CHURCH ELECT THANKS PRESS

Like Paper That Does Not Deny Columns to Lowly

A rising vote of thanks to the Spokane Press was taken by the entire congregation of the Church Elect in the healing tents at Ash and Chelan Monday night.

The resolution to which the congregation signified their approval was read from the pulpit. It follows:

"Resolved that the entire congregation by a rising vote expresses our thanks to the editor and staff of the Spokane Press for the impartial reports of these divine healing and teaching meetings and express our gratification because there is one newspaper in Spokane that cannot be intimidated by the influential, nor which will deny its columns to the lowly."

John G. Lake in Spokane

The following is a letter drafted to the faithful from John G. Lake.

THE CHURCH AT PORTLAND
129 Fourth St.
Portland, Ore., Aug. 1, 1924

TO EVERYONE WITHIN THE CIRCLE OF OUR INFLUENCE:

The Church at Portland sends greetings in Jesus name. As is known to all, our beloved Overseer has been absent in Spokane for some time where he is conducting a great Divine Healing tent meeting. The following letter from him tells the story of the battle to date.

Spokane, Wash., July 29, 1924.

Beloved in Christ Jesus our Lord:

With gratitude to God we write this letter. The battle has been fierce and heavy, but we praise God for wonderful victory. The challenge of the powers of darkness has been met at every turn until the guns and thunders of the enemy have been silenced. When our Christ and His power to save and heal was denied by newspapers and medical rings, in the name of our Christ we boldly challenged through the Press of the city the medical fraternity, in the interests of truth

Fire of God

and righteousness, to appoint a committee composed of one member from each of the different schools of medical practice to select fifty incurables, permit us to minister to them for thirty days, then let the doctors examine them again, and if numbers were not satisfactorily and permanently healed we would pay $500.00 into any charity fund the committee would suggest.

This challenge has gone around the press of the nation. God honored the boldness of this stand for God by an immediate sun-burst of healing power, so that the enemies of God were instantly discomfited.

We desire to thank every precious child of God who labored in faith and prayer for and with us in this glorious battle and victory. The unusual interest of the public can be understood when we call attention to the fact that our tent meetings have held their place as front page news for over four weeks, and the Spokane Press reports over 500 new subscriptions to their paper as the result of the meetings.

We do not desire you to feel that this is a finished victory. No, oh no! The battle has only begun. Beloved, what religious meeting in Portland has been able to hold a place as front page news for two days, let alone for over four weeks? This city is stirred, God is honored. Pray, oh pray for God's power to bind the bundles and harvest the whitened fields that have ripened through the tears, the sorrows and prayers of God's faithful saints.

Beloved, set aside an hour each day when you go alone before God and pray for His love and power on my soul, and the souls of all who labor with me in the gospel. Pray for the Holy Ghost to convict and save the people. Gather a group of friends and neighbors to pray. Attend the meetings and encourage the Church to pray. How we need God here to gather the results of this glorious Holy Ghost message and ministry into the granary of God that Jesus Christ may "see the travail of his soul and be satisfied."

I am deeply longing to be in Portland, where by God's grace we trust to inaugurate a campaign for God, just as soon as the hot weather has passed. Pray for Portland. The city of St. Joe, Idaho is also calling for help, reporting that not a religious service is maintained in the city. The churches stand vacant while the devil runs loose in the streets.

Beloved, gather in the tithes. Be true to God. This blessing on the city of Spokane has been born in the prayer life of The Church at Portland. We feel that the prayers and tears of The Church at Portland has availed for the Church here, but oh beloved, do not permit the devil to rob Portland of the glory and blessing that is hers through laxness or carelessness at the very last moment. Beware of scattering your power, or dissipating the precious presence of the Spirit, or grieving the blessed Holy Ghost upon whose presence and assistance all our hopes depend.

It delights my heart to hear of blessing of God upon our Brother LeDoux in your midst in salvation and healing. Stand under him with your prayers. Bring in your tithes and offerings. Let the house of God not be found empty, not the <u>treasury empty</u>, but may our God behold with delight a faithful congregation, waiting, praying, laboring until the glory of God comes. "Bring ye all the tithes into the store house, and PROVE ME saith the Lord of Hosts." Prove Him, prove Him, prove Him!

Your Brother in Christ,
JOHN G. LAKE, Overseer

John G. Lake

John G. Lake in Spokane

Thursday, August 7, 1924 The Spokane Press

HEALED BY GOD PARADE STREETS

Expect 250 members of the Church Elect to enter.

In what they hope will be an impressive testimony to the power of God to heal, about 250 persons who claim to have been healed of their diseases through prayer will parade on the downtown streets Saturday afternoon, August 16, at 3 o'clock. A permit for the use of 50 automobiles, and a band, to parade at that time has been issued to Dr. John G. Lake, head of the Church Elect, by the city council. In speaking of the parade today, Lake said; "We believe in testifying to the power of God at every opportunity. It is not possible to get the message we have to teach before everyone. We believe that when the citizens of Spokane see this group of persons, many of them once at death's door with incurable diseases, that it will be a forceful and unforgettable testimony that God does heal."
The regular Thursday night healing meeting will be held in the tents at Ash and Chelan at 8 o'clock.

Fire of God

Monday, August 18, 1924 The Spokane Press

HEALED BY GOD PARADE TOWN

50 autos carrying 250 persons healed by Lake's prayers. Thousands of Spokane persons witnessed the unique parade of "healed" persons from the "Church Elect," when they rode through downtown streets in automobiles Saturday afternoon. About 50 automobiles Saturday were in line, more than 250 persons who claim to have been healed of all manner of diseases by the power of God were in the cars.

The automobiles were placarded with signs which told of the diseases from which the occupants were cured. The cures effected by the prayers of Dr. John G. Lake according to the signs were: Nervous prostration, pneumonia, diabetes, paralysis, tuberculosis, adenoids, shingles, flu, eczema, leakage of the heart, rheumatism, and broken arches.

The feature of the parade was a delivery car containing more than a dozen children, and which bore the sign, "born painlessly" on each side . The mothers of these children have no assistance in childbirth other than prayer, they declare.

Dr. John G. Lake preceded by a band, led the parade. The cars traveled downtown streets for more than an hour.

Personal Glimpses

Personal Glimpses

John Graham Lake

Birth date: March 18, 1870
Birth place: St. Mary's, Ontario, Canada
Height: 5'11"
Weight: 190 in 1935
Eyes: Grey; wore bifocals on occasion
Marital status: Feb. 1893 married Jennie Stevens, who died in Africa. On Nov 27, 1913 married Florence Switzer
Date of death: Sept. 16, 1935
Place of burial: Riverside Memorial Park

The following personal glimpses of John G. Lake were the offerings of those who knew Dr. Lake either as members of his church or those who had received ministry. All of these people were interviewed at length. Some of these dear saints are no longer with us, but their memories remain. I have chosen not to alter the conversational tone of these remembrances. It is important to hear the words from those who spoke them.

John G. Lake in Spokane

"I Was There"

Testimony by
Clark Peterson- church member

As I recall, most of his preaching was about how great our God is. What He is able to do in His healing. John Lake just commanded an audience. He would build up faith in you to believe what God can do and what He will do.

Lake was a wonderful man. He commanded respect. It was just his nature. What he had to say people took 100% because of his ability to speak and convey what the Lord was speaking to him. He was magnificent.

He would take on anyone, anytime, anywhere. He took on the Spokesman Review and so forth and he was natural because he was an editor himself. When it came to that they couldn't trip him up or anything else.

I believe that someplace it talks about he was trying to find out something by the Spirit by some machine. They had a machine of some kind and they wanted to test him to see something about the Spirit and he'd just say bless the Lord and then he'd say bless the Lord again. That machine would go so high is just couldn't go any higher. Just getting the "radiation of the Spirit." They tested it on neutral but when he started to bless the Lord and then go deeper and deeper that thing couldn't register it.

He wasn't a man especially for show, but if you really needed a proof of the real thing, he would never back down or anything. He would come out on top, because he was a man of faith.

Fire of God

He was a man of means at one time but he gave that up. Lake was a man of education and so forth, so he was well in command of his vocabulary and he put things across and he had no fear. He was like a lion.

The Meeting Place......... It was the Rookery Building and the entrance came in from Sprague Avenue. There was Fogwell and Westwood. Westwood was one of the main ones about that time. And they set up what they called the healing rooms and they had church there just about all day. The people would come in that were sick and needed help. Lake had a room and Westwood had one.

If people were not familiar with divine healing it would depend upon how urgent their condition was and how they felt about getting into the Spirit. God would heal them. They just kept coming back every day or whenever they felt like it. Those rooms were open and men were praying for them and there were others who took over, and between praying for them, why they had services there, teaching them faith and were able to get them healing.

We had a large orchestra in the church, and we sang songs like "All Hail King Jesus." I remember when they were downtown and were having meetings at the Masonic Temple and we would go down there. It was a big building there and entered from Riverside, it was very large. Many people came to the meetings and received their healing through the ministry. Whenever someone needed help, Lake was there to help them. People aren't as pessimistic when they see that they can get help. Then they are ready to bend to do what it takes to get their healing.

I remember Lake telling a story of a native preacher in Africa named Letwaba. Letwaba had come to a place where he needed to cross a river, and he just found himself across the

John G. Lake in Spokane

river, doing the work of the Lord. They asked him how he got there. He didn't know. He was translated. He had to cross the river and the Lord took him over to the other side.

Oh Yes, there have been a great amount of people brought to Christ through Lake's ministry.

I tell you, the things that man had to go through, he was stubborn and strong. Naturally he had a strong spirit. God really picked a man that had something that was not wishy-washy. Not up one day and down the next. It was just something in his character. He could up and give everything away. When he went to Africa he didn't even have enough money, but God sent him that far, so he had faith. The fire of God burned in his soul, Praise God.

In the early days boy, you couldn't talk about anything Pentecostal. Speaking in tongues and so forth without having people fight you for it.

All my Christian learning is based on foundational teachings of John G. Lake. I started when I was only eight years old and I am 82 now. So I had been under a lot of teaching, so has my family, my wife and children and her side of the family.

We have been in many dire positions, many times and God has come through and answered prayer. The impossible, God did it. Praise God, Hallelujah.

John Lake was a man who was able to stand up. He could speak intelligently to the forces of the enemy. He could speak to the people in papers and editorials and in fact, he enjoyed it. He actually wrote editorials in the paper, quite regularly. He had a lot of opposition, but he put them in.

When you get isolated out in a field by yourself and the devil is hooking you, you need to get hold of the Lord.

Lake's ministry helped my family. Let me tell you. We lived up at a ranch near Diamond Lake, just this side of

Fire of God

Newport. Morris Moser who married my mother's sister got diphtheria.

My nephew got it also and he died; he was just a baby, 3 or 4 years old. They sent a sheriff and a quarantine officer out there and quarantined their home. My dad and I, we stayed together at the ranch which was 1 ½ miles away and I started to feel something in my throat too.

I hitched up the team of horses after dark, because we didn't have a car, and we were suppose to go to Newport, which had the nearest phone and call Spokane for help, because we thought we were going to be quarantined too. I got to town and called the Spokane church. I got a hold of somebody and told them we needed prayer. I was praying and testifying to this young fellow. We needed help and we got help. I had victory over this problem, I had it before I got home. It was either life or death in times like that.

There was Lake, Fogwell, and Westwood. Westwood was one of the main ones at the time, and they set up what they called the healing rooms and they had church there just about all day, and the people would come in that were sick and needed help. Those men hardly ever got their own clothes off, round the clock, praying for thousands. There were miracles then.

Rev. Fogwell was out ministering in the Model T, they are the most cantankerous things to drive. Well after turning a corner, it turned over on him and the Lord raised it right off of him.

I remember during the time of the flu epidemic, they would quarantine houses, not for the flu but for other things, and Lake wasn't afraid of them. He would go around to the back door and get in somehow to pray for them people and come out. They were healed time after time when he went out. This was really some ministry, it started small but as you have probably read, it finished big.

John G. Lake in Spokane

Ray Ferguson - Husband of Edna Lake

Remembering John G. Lake

John G. Lake was born in Canada, he was a carpenter, he moved to the United States to Newberry, Michigan, where he met Jennie Wallace Stevens. They got married and moved to Sault Sainte Marie, Michigan, where he went into the real estate and insurance business. The business prospered and John became very wealthy. It was during this time that he felt a calling to enter the missionary field.

In 1908 Lake was told by God that he was ready to go on a mission. Lake knew that if he went and did what he was taught to do, that the finances would always be available. John booked passage for Capetown, Africa. Upon arriving at Capetown, the ship was met by a lady who directed them to Johannesburg, where John established his church. His mission did well in Johannesburg and after it was well established he started moving into the back country to establish native churches and had good progress.

John kept going further into the interior establishing churches. After one was established, he would put someone in charge and move on to the next one.

One of the highlights that happened was when the home church would send out bundles of clothing to the mission.

In the end it was said that he established about 500 native churches.

Lake's wife died and he moved back to the United States.

Fire of God

When John got to Spokane in 1914 he started a church which he called, "The Church at Spokane."

He had gotten a home on the north side and had married Florence Switzer. Florence was a really nice person.

He continued in his ministry there with a time in Portland as well as in California and Texas. He returned to Spokane in late 1931 and pastored until his death in 1935.

> **"Divine Healing of Spirit, Soul and Body"**
>
> The very core of real religion.
> The highest expression of union with Christ.
> Wonderful testimonies of revealing the power of God.
>
> **Sunday Services at Knights of Pythias Temple**
>
> Corner Riverside and Jefferson.
>
> **11 a. m. and 3 p. m.**
>
> Healing Rooms, 340 Rookery Bldg.   Phone Main 1463.
>
> JOHN G. LAKE, Overseer.

John G. Lake in Spokane

Alice Fritsch Interview
Remembering John G. Lake

You never grew tired of hearing him speak. Some of his services would last a long time.

About his wife, Florence, she was simply tremendous. She would sit down in that front row. My brothers would just love to sit by her. They watched her take shorthand of every sermon.

When he would ask her to pray, it was just wonderful. She lived very close to the Lord. She was never down, she would never complain but was always on top.

We kids would go over to the Lake house down on West Indiana. John, although he may not have hardly a penny in his pocket seemed to have enough to buy a big old watermelon for all the kids.

You can ask all five of my brothers. Those were the best years of our lives.

Lake had lots of lung power. When he would pray and stomp his foot, he really could fill the whole building with his voice. He was a big, powerful man. He didn't need loudspeakers like they do today, where everyone has a microphone.

He would shout, he was sure to be heard. We have lots of good memories. The people in the church were very enthusiastic.

When Lake was down at the Masonic Temple there were a lot of young people down there. They had quite a group, even at that time.

John Lake was great at giving out money to those who needed it, but he could discern right then if it was for real. If it wasn't he would chop that right off. He would tell them that they were insincere.

I think what touched me the most about John Lake was his generosity. He never kept a thing for himself. Even the humble home they lived in impressed me. His wife handled their home very well. A minister's wife can either make or break a minister. She was a blessing to all of us. She was such a strong testimony of his great work.

Many times during prayer, John Lake would come down in the audience. One Sunday night we missed because of transportation, John prayed for a blind girl and her eyes were opened.

The church community as a whole were in unity. The press mostly seemed positive in their articles.

Lake was mostly well received in Spokane. Our time at Lake's church taught us faithfulness. It really has never left us. I am so glad that I lived in the days when we had such strong ministers of the word.

John G. Lake in Spokane

Ione Eaton Interview
August 26, 1990
Remembering John G. Lake

My parents met in his church when they were young people going there. I remember when I was very small, the meetings were deeply impressive to me. He would have afternoon meetings and people of all churches he invited, where ever he went, and on Sunday afternoons many people from other groups would come and fellowship, and then go to their own churches on Sunday nights. The building was always just packed every Sunday. People were just standing all around. When they got together something really happened, that wasn't happening in their own organized church groups. And one of the things that impressed me very much among the young people was that the Spirit of the Lord was there and would touch these young people and they would be slain under the power without being touched.

The platform was full of musical instruments. They had two big xylophones, boys and girls playing the instruments. I remember one beautiful tall girl playing the trombone. There was anointing in the music those young people were playing. The young people's services were very special to me, and I do remember Livingstone Lake ministering to the young people before he was married.

I feel the mantle of Brother Lake fell on many people who are scattered all around. In fact, I feel the impact of his ministry, in my own heart today very deeply. I have transferred that to my children.

This vision that Brother Lake had, had a profound impact in healing, and with touching peoples lives.

Fire of God

When I was sick my mom would call him. Once my brother broke his arm, and he was instantly healed. We were playing tag as kids and he fell over a bannister of a porch and his wrist just snapped. I could hear the pop. He was in severe pain and my dad had a bicycle and he took him on his bicycle to the Tabernacle on Lincoln and Sharp on a Wednesday night. They were just starting to let out service, and they took Albert up there and told Brother Lake what had happened. Brother Lake put his hands up and told everyone to stop what they were doing, and said "agree with me for this one. This little boy has a broken arm." They ministered to him and the pain stopped instantly, and daddy brought him back home on the bicycle, he was able to sleep that night. We really did rejoice.

He also prayed for my sister who had a concussion. We called him out to the house. He asked, "Did this girl have a bad fall?" And we said yes. She couldn't stand or walk or anything. She was vomiting and he finally said, "Let's pray." He would say Bless God a lot. He just started right then in coming against the principalities. He ministered to her and she was healed instantly. She was able to walk and start to eat. He also cast out all the fears and doubts.

Then my dad, he ran away as a boy. His mother passed away and his step-mother didn't get along with him very well so they put him in an orphanage and he ran away.

His father went to Brother Lake and asked him to pray that his boy would get in touch with him. My daddy had a vision of Jesus. In it, Jesus opened his arms to him, and then the first thing he wanted to do was write his father. This was told over the radio, I remember hearing it, as a little girl. He used to be on about fifteen minutes, every day about noon in the thirties, and he told how the Lord sent a runaway boy home.

He was very, very impressive. He had a strong spirit, not a strong-willed spirit, but just like a father or a grandfather.

John G. Lake in Spokane

He used to sit me in his lap and tell me a lot of the missionary stories that happened in Africa.

I can say that no man has ever had a more profound effect on my life than John G. Lake, and I have known many great ministers.

He was not dictated to by an organized group.

He encouraged the people to seek the Lord always, in their "closets," and to depend on the Lord for every need. He was very much against doctors, he felt that the Lord created these bodies and he knew more about us than any doctor. He felt that God could take care of those needs.

My grandfather took my mother to the healing rooms. She was very sick with inflammatory rheumatism, and she was just a teenage girl. So they took her into the prayer rooms. Brother Lake prayed for her. She had such a miraculous healing. It was a total healing of her body.

He very much inspired me during my school years. I had a deep sense of trusting the Lord. I, to this day don't go to a doctor for anything. The Lord has met with me and my children because of something planted in me. A seed planted in me to trust the Lord.

Many things happened in the raising of my own children. I many times fell to my knees in prayer and God came through.

There was a prostitute who was saved; brought to the Lord and she came to the Tabernacle. I remember her very strongly because she wore a lot of heavy make-up and wore real bright clothes. In those days everybody was more conservative. Some of the older ladies got a hold of her and told her she had to change her ways of dress and not put make-up on. Some of the brethren saw this and went to Brother Lake and told him what was happening. I was there when he did this. So up on the platform, he started talking about how the Lord had saved this woman and cleaned her up inside and he talked to these ladies and said, "You old hens, you keep your hands off of her, the Lord has cleaned her upon the inside and He can take care of the outside." He was very emphatic about always letting the Lord do the work.

He would go downtown and minister to people and pray for them right on the street. It didn't bother him when people would stand and look.

Lake encouraged the people to press into the Spirit and to walk close to the Lord. He was responsible for bringing many homes back together with God's help. Many times when husbands and wives were ready to split up he would speak truth into the situation. He had a tremendous counseling ministry.

I had a sore throat, it was worse than strep throat. He called me up to the platform. He said, "girlie, come up here." He had me open my mouth. He said this is the worse case of septic sore throat he had ever seen. He laid hands on me and prayed for me. I wasn't healed instantly, but within two days I was completely healed. My parents didn't let me go out when I was sick, they didn't take me to the doctor, but they would take me to church.

I remember he would tell new Christians to read the book of John. He felt that it had much in it to encourage the new Christian

The last time I saw Brother Lake was at a church picnic at Mission Park. The ladies were getting dinner ready. He came up to me and said to the ladies, "this girl looks hungry to me, you fix her a sandwich right now." It kind of embarrassed me. He had me sit down and made those ladies give me a sandwich. It was that night, that he had his stroke.

John G. Lake in Spokane

Letter mailed on November 15, 1989
From: L. G. Lake
To: Brett Wyatt

Personal information about John G. Lake as remembered by his son, Jack (L.G.). Jack is the eldest of 5 children by John's second wife. Two sisters and Jack are still living.

John liked to take the family to places he had been. One favorite was from Kennewick to Umatilla, Oregon. Before the highway was paved, they would take the ferry across the Columbia River, up the Columbia River highway to Pasco (via Wallula Junction) and then home.

People called him day and night to come pray for them. He drove many miles to their homes.

His wife would send him to the market for groceries but by the time he got home, he had given much to less fortunate people he met. He was very generous.

Many times he invited guests for dinner without telling his wife. Many times she had to change the menu because what she had planned to have would not serve the extra guests.

The 5 children would crawl in bed with their dad on Sunday mornings and he would read the "funnies" to them. Then he would listen to them tell of their activities. (Especially if he had been on a preaching stint for a few weeks)

The family moved from Spokane (where Jack was born) to Portland. Then to San Diego, Houston, Texas and Oakland, California. John lost his voice for a time. At that time his 2 eldest sons (by 1st wife) and he sold advertising for a newspaper.

When John's voice healed, the family moved back to Portland, Oregon. In 1932 they moved back to Spokane. In 1933 he bought the "frame tabernacle" on Lincoln and Sharp.

The Critics

The Critics

Dr. John G. Lake never had to look for critics. As he preached the God anointed word to the masses of people, there were always those who didn't believe it and who would speak against it. Included in this chapter when possible are the statements and some biographical information about those persons who challenged the credibility of Dr. Lake's ministry. This is followed in each case by John G. Lake's response. A notation has been made at the top of each page to differentiate between Lake's words and those of the critics.

John G. Lake in Spokane

CRITIC

Reverend F.E. Beatty;
Minister of Lidgerwood Presbyterian Church in Spokane

Spokane Chronicle Monday January 17, 1916

HEALING BY FAITH CAN'T BE EXPECTED

Human Agency is Necessary, Declares Minister of Lidgerwood Church.

"Healing by divine power, exclusive of human agencies, can not be expected more than people expect to have their physical wants supplied in answer to prayer for daily bread if they fail to sow and reap and labor with their hands," said Rev. F. E. Beatty of the Lidgerwood Presbyterian church in his Sunday morning sermon on "Divine Healing."

He said in part:"Jesus said to his disciples: 'As the Father hath sent me, even so send I you.' Jesus' work may be summed up under three general heads— preaching, teaching and healing. The church therefore is to preach the truths of eternal salvation and eternal punishment, teach the word of God that men may know the Scriptures which will make them wise unto salvation, and also make known the fact that sick are not to be neglected."

"I believe in the power of prayer and believe that some have been healed through prayer, but I also know that many are not healed who have faith in God and pray for healing and have others pray for them. Paul, the greatest apostle of the early church, sought God for help because of an infirmity, but he was not healed or given relief."

Healing Gift of Spirit

"Paul tells us of the different gifts of the spirit, one of which is healing. All people do not have all of these gifts of the

Fire of God

spirit. Not long ago one who advertises himself as a healer said in a sermon which I heard said: 'Any and every one can have the gift of healing.' This statement and Paul's statement do not seem to agree.

"We must recognize at least three forms of healing. Mental or psychic, divine healing, and remedial healing. The Bible recognizes all three of these forms of healing. We may therefore use the three. The use of one does not exclude the other."

"We pray for the kingdom of God to come and are to go out and teach the laws of God's kingdom. We also pray for daily bread and in spite of many instances of miraculous feeding in the Bible we do not sit down and wait for God to hand us bread and meat, but plant and reap or labor with our hands to earn that which will buy bread."

No Sign of Disbelief.

"We pray, 'Forgive us our debts as we forgive our debtors.' We have our part to do in answering our own prayers. We do not limit God, but recognize that he is able to work for healing through men of science as he works through men for the accomplishment of other of his purposes."

"Our making use of good nursing, cleanliness, cheerfulness and a good physician is not then a sign of lack of faith, but a sign that we recognize that God is able to perform miracles of healing through his agents just as he performs every day miracles of grace unto salvation through his loyal servants."

John G. Lake in Spokane

Lake's reply to Rev. F. E. Beatty

In the Spokane Daily Chronicle of January 17th, there appeared a condensed report of a sermon by the Reverend F. E. Beatty of the Lidgerwood Presbyterian Church. The article is headlined "Healing by Faith Can't Be Expected."

The article presents so much absurdity that it is difficult to imagine that it was actually delivered to an intelligent congregation.

The reverend gentleman stated that Jesus said to His disciples, "As my Father hath sent me, even so send I you."

"Jesus' work may be summed up under three general heads, preaching, teaching, and healing," he says. "The church, therefore, is to preach the truths of eternal salvation and eternal punishment. Teach the word of God that men may know the Scriptures, which will make them wise unto salvation, and also make known the fact that the sick are not to be neglected."

He states the fact of Jesus' ministry as teaching and preaching and healing. He quotes the words of Jesus, "As the Father hath sent me. Even so send I you." Nobody with sense could imagine that the disciples were sent to do anything else than what Jesus had done, in the manner He had done it. Is the disciple going to accomplish by another method different from the method of Jesus, the thing Jesus sent him to do? If the sick are to be healed, then we must discover how Jesus healed and how the disciples healed. In Luke 9:1-6, we distinctly read that "He called unto him his twelve disciples and gave them power and authority over all devils, and to cure diseases, and sent them to preach the kingdom of God and heal the sick."

He did not present them with a medicine kit. He sent them with the conscious power of God upon their lives, with spiritual dominion over sickness and demon powers. The Scriptures abound with healings through the ministry of the apostles. There is no question in any intelligent mind as to what the method was.

In connection with the revival in the city of Samaria, it is distinctly recorded in Acts 8:6-7,

> The people with one accord gave heed unto those things which Philip spake, hearing and seeing the miracles which he did. For unclean spirits, crying with loud voice, came out of many that were possessed with them: and many taken with palsies, and that were lame were healed.

These healings took place, not at the hands of the original twelve, to whom the power had first been given, but now at the hands of a new disciple, Philip.

The reverend gentleman says further, "I believe in the power of prayer, and I believe that some have been healed through prayer. Paul the greatest apostle of the early church besought God for help because of an infirmity, but he was not healed or given relief." We would like to inquire what this statement is based upon. If we can read the Scriptures correctly, certainly Paul was healed. He had prayed three times. He was not healed the first time, nor the second time, but he prayed the third time and declares that the Lord said to him, " Paul my grace is sufficient for you."

Surely the grace of God is sufficient for every man. It was sufficient for Paul's needs too. The assertions that he was not healed is one of the centuries-old theological jokes. Does our reverend friend expect a 1916 audience to believe that Paul was not healed when he prayed?

Again, there is not the least evidence in the Scriptures that he needed any healing. What his "thorn in the flesh" was is a pure conjecture. One thing we know, Paul was not only

John G. Lake in Spokane

healed himself when blind, through the laying on of the hands of Ananias, but that he himself healed others.

On his way to Rome when his ship was wrecked, he healed the father of the governor of the island, and many others. The assertion that he was not healed himself is almost as stale an argument as the reference to Luke as the beloved physician. Jesus was a beloved physician too. So were each of the apostles. So is any man who brings healing to the sick. There is not the least evidence in the Scriptures that Luke ever owned a medicine kit in his life, and if he did, he most certainly left it behind when he accepted the ministry and power of the Lord Jesus Christ.

Our land is filled with men who have been physicians and who have abandoned the practice for the better way and method of the Lord Jesus Christ. Dr. Finnis B. Yoakum, of Los Angeles, California, one of the leading physicians of his city, abandoned his practice of medicine and adopted the ministry of healing through the prayer of faith and the laying on of hands, as the superior method. Dr. W.D. Gentry, of Chicago, a writer on diagnosis, whose treatise on the subject are found in every first-class library, abandoned the practice of medicine and for years has ministered in the name of Jesus, through the prayer of faith and laying on of hands as Jesus commanded. Likewise Dr. A.B. Simpson of New York, a leading osteopath, abandoned his practice of medicine, and many others.

Each one of these are "beloved physicians," but they do not give pills. They have graduated into the higher way.

What a strange thing it is when Christian ministers are found endeavoring to dodge the real issue of healing, instead of building up faith in God. In many cases, they are among the first to endeavor to break it down and try and explain away by some cunning method the real plain facts of the Scriptures. How much more honorable it would be if ministers would acknowledge, as they should, that Christ has not changed, that

Fire of God

faith is the same quality it ever was, but that they do not possess it and so are not able to secure answers to prayer for the sick. Reverend Andrew Murray, the head of the Dutch Reform Church of South Africa, whose books are throughout all Christendom and who is generally recognized as one of the saints of this age, was dying of an incurable throat disease. The physicians of Africa gave him no hope. He came to London, England, but received no hope from the medical men there. He went to Bagster's Bethsan Divine Healing Home and was perfectly healed.

He returned to South Africa and wrote a book on the subject of healing, and it was placed on sale by the church. After a little while, the ministers of the Dutch Reform Church discussed it in conferences. They said, "If we leave this book in circulation the people will read it. Then the next thing we know they will ask us to pray the prayer of faith that saves the sick, and we have not the faith to do it, and our jobs will be in danger." So it was decided to withdraw the book from circulation.

Why not give the people the light of the scriptures? Let them know that Jesus is the healer still, that He empowers men today through the Holy Spirit, to heal the sick, just as He ever did. That the Spirit of God is not obtained through the Church, but that it comes upon the soul of man, straight from God Himself when necessary hundredfold consecration is made.

John G. Lake

John G. Lake in Spokane

Who Was Dr. E.J. Bulgin   CRITIC

Dr. Bulgin was a world renowned Bible lecturer. He was well known for a lecture which he gave in Spokane at St. Paul's Methodist Church, which denounced John G. Lake and others which had the same ministry. He had been quoted as saying in his lectures "that the lectures would burn up the infidels, their standards and their cults." More often than not, when Bulgin referred to Lake and his followers, those very same words, (infidels and cults) were used regularly.

It seems rather odd that this would come from a man who was quoted as saying on February 16, 1920, "that the world has no confidence in a trimmed down gospel." It is an inconsistency to say in one sentence to preach the gospel as it ought to be, and in the next to, defame those people which were doing just that.

Lake was not intimidated by this challenge or any other challenge given to him by man. He knew the secret to his strength, was Jesus Christ and he had personal assurance by the Lord Jesus that he was preaching the true gospel of Jesus Christ. The following pages include Lake's reply to the worldwide evangelist and Bible lecturer, Dr. E.J. Bulgin.

Fire of God

Lake's Reply to Bulgin

Spokane, Washington, February 28th, 1920

Dr. Elwood Bulgin,
Spokane, Washington.

Dear Brother in Christ:
 It was my privilege to be present at your meeting at the St. Paul Methodist Church at Spokane last Monday night and listen to your sermon. I was deeply impressed by the masterful manner in which you marshaled your facts, and the spirit in which they were presented to your great audience.
 Your presentation of the deity of Jesus Christ, and the sharpness with which you brought the facts of the denial of the deity of Jesus by the Christian Scientists, were striking. The masterful handling of the whole subject commanded my admiration, and I believe the admiration of a great majority of your audience.
 Men can speak with frankness to each other, particularly when their interest in the Kingdom of Jesus Christ is identical. You have lived, loved, and denied yourself, and suffered for the cause of the Kingdom of Christ in the earth. I, too, have loved and suffered for my fidelity to the vision of the redemption of Jesus Christ which God revealed to me.
 For twenty-five years I have labored, as few men in the world have labored for so long a period, to bring before the world as far as I could the magnificent truths of the redemptive blood and life and power of the Son of God.
 Your methods and my methods have been different. You in your forceful, philosophical manner, have undertaken to destroy faith in Christian Science through opposition, ridicule, and exposure of what you believe to be its fallacies. On the other hand, I have undertaken by specific revelation of the truth

John G. Lake in Spokane

of Jesus Christ concerning the healing power of God, and its availability for all men today, to show the world that there is no need for any man to leave any stable Christian body in order to secure the benefits of salvation and healing specifically declared by Jesus Christ Himself to be available for every man.

Jesus, in contrast with the ancient philosophers and reformers of the past and present, first gave Himself in consecration to God, body, soul, and spirit-- thereby establishing the pattern consecration for all Christians forever. His baptism was the dedication and commitment of Himself "unto all righteousness." He undertook to reveal the righteousness of God. Note the nature of this revelation.

Having definitely committed Himself, His body, His soul, His spirit, to God forever, immediately there descended upon Him the witness to His hundredfold consecration. The Holy Ghost came from heaven as a dove and abode upon Him, as it ever will upon every man who will meet Almighty God with the same utterances of real consecration to God, of spirit and soul and body. This reveals the demand of God upon the Christians' person and conscience, and the answer of God from heaven to this fullness of consecration.

Being thus definitely equipped, He proceeded to the wilderness for testing by Satan, to see if this consecration of body and soul and spirit would endure.

He overcame all the efforts of Satan to tempt Him in the specific departments of His life: first, the body; second, the soul; third, the spirit. He overcame, through reliance on God and His word, and came forth in the power of the Spirit. He announced the constructive platform of His life and ministry, containing the following six planks:

The Spirit of the Lord is upon me,
because He hath anointed me.
First--To preach the gospel to the poor.
Second--He hath sent me to heal the broken hearted.

Fire of God

Third--To preach deliverance to the captives.
Fourth--Recovering of sight to the blind.
Fifth--To set at liberty them that are bruised.
Sixth--To preach the acceptable year of the Lord.

    God's acceptable year had come. No more waiting for the year of Jubilee and all its consequent blessings. God's never ending Jubilee was at hand in Jesus Christ.

    He then went throughout all Galilee teaching in their synagogues, and preaching the gospel of the Kingdom, and healing all manner of sickness and all manner of disease among the people, and so established forever the ideal of Christian ministry for the Church of God.

    Then He empowered twelve men, and "sent them to preach the Kingdom of God, and to heal the sick." Profiting by their experience, and advancing in faith and knowledge of the power of God, He "called seventy others also." But in sending forth the seventy, He reversed the order of instruction. To the seventy He said: "Go into the cities round about. Heal the sick that are therein, and say to them, The Kingdom of God is come nigh unto you." And they returned rejoicing that even the devils were subject to them "through thy name."

    Then came His wonderful entrance into death, His redemption on the cross, His resurrection from the grave, His interviews with His disciples, His last commission in which, according to Mark, He established in the Church of Christ, to be born through their preaching in all the world, the very same ministry of salvation and healing that He Himself during His earth life had practiced. That ministry contained the message of Jesus to all the world and the anointing with power from on high, just as He had received it at His baptism. Indeed He commanded them to wait in Jerusalem until "Ye shall be baptized with the Holy Ghost, not many days hence."

John G. Lake in Spokane

He declared to them that certain signs should follow, saying: "These signs shall follow them that believe. Every one, every Christian soul was thus commissioned by Jesus to heal the sick and sinful from sickness and

In my name shall they--
First--Cast out devils.
Second--They shall speak with new tongues.
Third--They shall take up serpents.
Fourth--And if they drink any deadly
things it shall not hurt them.
Fifth--They shall lay hands on the sick
and they shall recover.

The same Holy Spirit of God which flowed through Jesus Christ, the anointing that was upon Him and which flowed through His hands and into the sick, was an impartation of God so real that when the woman touched the hem of His garment she was conscious of the instant effect of the healing in her body through it. "She felt in her body that she was healed of that plague," while Jesus Himself was likewise conscious of an outflow. He said: "Somebody hath touched me, for I perceive that virtue is gone out of me."

Divine Healing is the particular phase of ministry in which the modern church does not measure up to the early church. This failure has been due to a real lack of knowledge of the real nature and the real process of Christian healing. The above incident reveals the secret of what the power was, how the power operated, and by what law it was transmitted from the disciple to the one who needed the blessing. The power was the Holy Ghost of God, both in Jesus Christ after His baptism in the Holy Ghost, and in the disciples after the baptism of the Holy Ghost came upon them on the day of Pentecost. It flowed through the hands of Jesus to the sick, it permeated the garments He wore. When the woman touched

Fire of God

even the hem of His garment there was sufficient of the power of God there for her need.

The disciples healed the sick by the same method. Indeed, the apostle Paul, realizing this law, permitted the people to bring to him handkerchiefs and aprons, that they might touch his body, and when they were carried to the sick, the sick were healed through the power of God in the handkerchiefs, and the demons that inhabited their persons went out of them.

Herein is shown the secret of the early church, that which explains the whole miracle-working power of the apostles and the early church for four hundred years. The same is evident in branches of the modern church. Herein is revealed the secret that has been lost. That secret is the conscious, tangible, living, incoming, abiding, outflowing Spirit of God, through the disciple of Christ who has entered into blood-washed relationship and baptism in the Holy Ghost.

This is the secret that the modern church from the days of the Reformation onward has failed to reveal. We have, however, retained a form of godliness, "but have denied the power thereof."

When Jesus laid His hands on people the Holy Ghost was imparted to them in healing virtue. When the disciples and early Christians likewise laid their hands on the sick, the Holy Ghost was imparted through them to the needy one. Likewise the Holy Ghost was imparted to preachers "for the work of the ministry," including healing. Primitive church history abounds in examples of healing in the same manner. Paul specifically enjoins Timothy to "forget not the gift *power* that is in thee, that came through the laying on of my hands." It was an impartation of the Holy Ghost to Timothy for the work of Christian ministry.

In the whole range of church history we have retained the form, but have lost its power, in a great degree. The Pope lays his hands on the head of the Bishops, the Bishop lays his

John G. Lake in Spokane

hands on the head of the Priest, the Priest lays his hands on the head of the communicants when he receives them as members of the church.

In the Protestant church in all her branches, the laying on of hands in ordination for the ministry is practiced. But in the early church it was not the laying on of hands alone, but through the laying on of hands the impartation of the definite living spirit of the living God, to the individual, took place. Through its power in him, he was constituted a real priest, a real elder, a real preacher with grace, healing power and faith anointed of God from on High.

God gave the blood of Jesus to the Christian Church. God gave the power of healing to the Christian Church in the Holy Ghost, and as long as they lived under the anointing of the Holy Ghost and exercised the faith of Jesus in their hearts, the healing power of God manifested and is still manifest where this condition exists. Christian Science exists because of the failure of the Christian Church to truly present Jesus Christ and His power through the Spirit, and minister it to the world.

Robert G. Ingersoll assailed the Holy Scriptures, laughed at the Christian God, destroyed the faith of men, wrecked their hopes and left them stranded, and abandoned amid the wreckage. Through this means, he brought the just condemnation of the world upon himself. The world condemns him to this hour in that he destroyed the faith of men without supplying to their souls something to take its place, as he should have done, and as any man who is honorable and true must do.

You recommended Divine Healing in one breath and denied its potency in the next. You have attacked Christian Science, the followers of Dowie, and others and arraigned them at the bar and condemned them, without giving to men a tangible way by which the healing of God might be brought to them. Why do you not study and practice Jesus Christ's own

Fire of God

way of healing and so make your ministry constructive? What are you going to do with the multitude of dying that the doctors can not help? Leave them to die: The doctors have got through with them. And in many instances even though they are still prescribing for them and are perfectly aware of their inability to heal the sick ones and are candid and willing to say so, Dr. Bulgin, what have you got for these? What have you given to these?

If a man were walking down the street with a very poor set of crutches and a ruffian came along and kicked the crutches from under him, and let him fall, every honest soul would rise in condemnation of the ruffian's act and demand reparation.

You come to the dying, kick their hope from under them, and let them fall to the ground, and leave them there to die without bringing them the true healing power in the blood and spirit of Jesus--it is not sufficient to say, "I believe in Divine healing"--if they are sick they must be healed.

This must not be construed as a defense of Christian Science. It is not given with that thought, nor in that spirit. It is given rather in the hope that as an influential man in the Christian Church, you may see the weakness of your position and of the position of the church, and by the grace of God call the Church back again to faith in Jesus Christ, the Son of God, for healing for every man from every disease as Jesus Christ intended it should be, and as the scriptures definitely, positively teach, and make proper scriptural provision for a definite healing ministry.

In the hope of supplying this need of the Church, the Protestant ministers of the city of Los Angeles have agreed in formal resolution to begin the teaching and study and practice of healing. How has this come to pass, and why? They have been whipped into it by the success of Christian Science.

John G. Lake in Spokane

A recent issue of a New York daily paper announces that the pastors of New York have likewise undertaken to teach the people the power of God to heal.

The Protestant Episcopal Church is endeavoring through the ministry of a layman of the Church of England from the old country, a Mr. Hickson, to educate their people in the truth of healing through the atonement of Jesus Christ, the Son of God, by the laying on of hands and the prayer of faith. In a few days the gentleman will appear at All Saints Cathedral, Spokane, for that purpose, and the sick will be invited to be ministered to in the name of the Son of God and healed through His blood purchase.

The Church of England in England and also in Africa, for ten years have been endeavoring to organize societies not to teach their people Christian Science, psychic therapeutics, or mental healing, all of which belong to the realm of the natural, but to teach and demonstrate the pure power of God from Heaven by the Holy Ghost, purchased by the blood of Jesus Christ, to heal diseases.

Frank N. Riale, a secretary of the Presbyterian Board of Education of New York, with sixty-three universities and colleges under his control and supervision, is the author of a remarkable book, "The Sinless, Sickless, Deathless Life," in which he recounts in a chapter entitled "How the light and the Fire Fell," the marvelous story of his own conversion. He was a minister of the gospel and a graduate of Harvard. He found his Lord at the hands of an Indian in Dakota. He tells of the light of God that came to his soul in sanctifying power through the ministry of a Salvation Army Officer, Col. Brengle. He relates his marvelous healing when a diseased and dying wreck, through the reading of a religious tract on healing and his experience in seeing many healed of all manner of diseases by the power of God. You are a Presbyterian, my Brother, you need not go out of your own Church for the truth of God concerning healing.

The question before the Church, now that the break toward healing has come, and it has come, is who is prepared to teach and demonstrate the truth of God concerning healing? Will it be a fact that in the absence of knowledge of God by the ministry of the church in her blindness and ignorance and helplessness be overwhelmed by Christian Science, New Thought and the thousand and one cults which teach psychological healing?

Where is the prophet of God who should come forward, teach and demonstrate the pure spiritual value and power of the Holy Ghost, secured for men because Jesus Christ, the Son of God, gave His blood to get it for them? Is it not time that such men as yourself arise in the dignity of Christ and throw off the shackles of formal religion, and by the grace of God enter into the real life of living power through the Son of God in the Holy Ghost, and rescue the church out of her present degradation; reestablishing forever Divine Healing on its true and scriptural basis, the atonement of Jesus Christ?

Twenty-five years ago the light concerning healing came to my soul, after four brothers and four sisters had died of diseases, and when four other members of the family were in a dying state, abandoned by the physicians as hopeless, and after my father had spent a fortune trying to obtain human help. One man of God who had the truth of God in his heart came to the rescue. All four sick ones were healed. I was an ardent Methodist. I loved my Church. My parents were members of an old Scotch Presbyterian Kirk. The Presbyterian Church had no light on the subject of healing; the Methodist Church had no light on the subject of healing. I received my light through a man who had been educated in the University of Edinburgh, and had been a minister of the Congregational Church. He knew the power of God to save, and the power of God to heal.

John G. Lake in Spokane

When I accepted this blessed truth and saw my family healed out of death, what was the attitude of the Church? Just what the attitude of all the leading churches has been. When I declared this truth before our conferences, she undertook to ostracize me; and from that day to this many of her ministry, who have prayed through to God and secured the blessing and power of God upon their soul to heal the sick, have been forced out of ministry.

Dr. Bulgin, it is time to quit attacking forms of faith, whether good or bad, and turn your attention and the attention of the church to the only thing that will deliver her out of her present wretchedness and inability to bless, and bring her back again to Christ, to the foot of the cross, to the blood of Jesus, to the Holy Ghost from on High, to the power of God and the real faith including healing, "once for all delivered to the saints." Through this Healing Ministry the Church at Spokane reports 100,000 healings by the power of God through five years of continuous daily efforts and the kindred blessed fact that the majority of those healed were saved from sin also.

The dying world is stretching out her hands for help. The Church on account of her laxness in this matter, opens the doors for the existence of Christian Science and all the thousand and one worn out philosophies that follow in her train. Let the manhood of the Church arise, take the place of the prophet of God, call her back to the ministry of real salvation. A blessed salvation not alone for men after they are dead, or that will give them bliss in heaven when they die, but to a salvation that gives eternal life in Christ, health for the mind, and the health for the body, and supplies likewise the power of God for the immediate need, for the need of the sick, for the need of the sinful, the wretched and dying and sin-cursed and disease-smitten.

Let the Church return in the glory of God and the Power of Christ to the original faith, as clearly demonstrated in the

New Testament; as perpetuated forever in the church through the nine gifts of the Holy Spirit, demonstrating beyond controversy that as long as the Holy Spirit is in the Church, so long are the gifts of the Holy Spirit not only present, but exercisable through faith.

(See 1st Corinthians 12th Chapter).

"For to one is given the Spirit.
First-The word of Wisdom.
Second-The word of Knowledge.
Third-Faith by the same spirit.
Fourth-The gifts of healing.
Fifth-The working of miracles.
Sixth-To another prophecy.
Seventh-To another discerning of spirits.
Eighth-To another divers kinds of tongues.
Ninth-To another the interpretation of tongues.

The unchanging order of government, spiritual enduement, and ministry of the gifts of the Spirit are further declared as follows: "And God hath set some in the church, first apostles, secondly prophets, thirdly teachers, after that miracles, then gifts of healing, helps, governments, diversities of tongues."

When the Church exercises these gifts then she may condemn Christian Science; Dowieism, or New Thought; then she may condemn every other philosophical cult; then she may condemn Unitarianism and everything also that you preach against. Though she will not need to. Jesus never did. There were just as many strange philosophies in His day as in ours. The constructive righteousness of Christ, the presence of the living Son of God to save and heal, the revelation to the world of His divine power, will stop the mouths of every ism, and manifest one glorious, triumphant, all-embracing power of God through Jesus Christ, His Son, and its everlasting superiority.

John G. Lake in Spokane

Neither will you be compelled as you glorify doctors, medicines, surgery, etc., when the greatest physicians on earth have deplored their inability to deliver the world from its cure of sickness. Then you can not only teach the theory of the atonement of our Lord and Savior Jesus Christ, but demonstrate its reality and power to save both soul and body.

All the abstract criticism in the world in powerless to stop the drift from the churches to Christian Science, so long as Christian Science heals the sick and the church does not. Men demand to be shown. When the authority of Jesus to forgive sins was challenged, He met the challenge with the healing of the palsied man, not with negations and criticisms. He said: "Whether it is easier to say, thy sins be forgiven thee; or to say, arise and walk?" But that ye may know... I say arise and walk. He was too big for abstract criticism. So must the Christian and the Church become.

Your Brother in Christ,

JOHN G. LAKE

Founder, Divine Healing Institute, Rookery Bldg., Spokane, Washington.

Fire of God

CRITIC
Who was Dr. Windell?

Dr. James Windell was listed in the Spokane directory as a Physician during the teens and twenties. He was one of the best known urologists in the northwest. Like many doctors of the era he seemed to have it in for the man who claimed that man could be healed by God instead of science. This idea of divine intervention seemed so foreign to doctors trained up for years in the practice of pure science to solve problems that many spoke out against Lake and his followers.

Doctors that worked with John G. Lake for a time, often began to see the results and became staunch supporters. In his sermons, Lake cites many doctors who became believers in the Power of God to heal.

Dr. Windell died in Spokane on December 20, 1932 in his office at the age of 70.

John G. Lake in Spokane

FROM LAKE'S REPLY TO DR. WINDELL
Sunday, April 25th, 1920

Doctors and Drugs

The public commonly believe that medicine is a great science, and that its practice is entirely scientific. Whereas, so great a man as Professor Douglas McGlaggen, who occupied the chair of Medical Jurisprudence in the University of Edinburgh, Scotland, declared: "There is no such thing as the science of medicine. From the days of Hippocrates and Galen until now we have been stumbling in the dark, from diagnosis to diagnosis, from treatment to treatment, and have not found the first stone on which to found medicine as a science."

Dr. James Mason Good of London, England, who was so eminent in his profession that for twenty-five years he had in his care the royal house of Britain, declared his convictions before the British Medical Association in these words: "The science of medicines is founded upon conjecture and improved by murder. Our medicines have destroyed more lives than all the war, pestilence, and famines combined."

The famous Professor Chauss of Germany, states with emphasis: "The common use of medicines for the curing of disease is unquestionably highly detrimental and destructive, and in my judgment is an agent for the creation of disease rather than its cure, in that through its use there is continuously set up in the human system abnormal conditions more detrimental to human life than the disease from which the patient is suffering."

Our own Dr. Holmes of Boston, formerly president of the Massachusetts Medical Association, said in an address before the Massachusetts Medical Association: "It is my conviction, after practicing medicine for thirty-five years, that if the whole Materia Medica were cast into the bottom of the

Fire of God

sea it would be all the better for mankind and all the worse for the fishes."

From these quotations from the heads of the medical profession in various countries, we perceive the power of the Word of God, which declares: "In vain shall they use many medicines. There is no healing for thee there."

Dr. John B. Murphy, the greatest surgeon our country has ever produced, has spoken his mind concerning SURGERY as follows: "Surgery is a confession of helplessness. Being unable to assist the diseased organ, we remove it. If I had my life to live over again, I would endeavor to discover preventative medicine, in the hope of saving the organ instead of destroying it."

Just prior to his death he wrote an article entitled "The Slaughter of the Innocents," condemning cutting out of tonsils and adenoids, demonstrating that the presence of inflammation and pus and the consequent enlargement was due to a secretion in the system that found lodgment in the tonsils and that the removal of the tonsils in no way remedied the difficulty, the poison being generated in the system. He purposed to give his knowledge to the public for their protection from useless operations that he regarded as criminal.

Passing of the Medicine Bottle

We are certainly making long strides forward when we read such words as these, and they concern us all because they concern our health. And it must be well borne in mind that the writer, Sir William Osler, M.D., is unquestionably the foremost living American physician and the highest authority on drugs in the medical world. He says what follows in the "Encyclopedia Americana."

"The new school does not feel itself under obligation to give any medicine whatever, while a generation ago not only

John G. Lake in Spokane

could few physicians have held their practice unless they did, but few would have thought it safe or scientific."

"Of course there are still many cases where the patient or the patient's friends must be humored by administering medicine, or alleged medicine, where it is not really needed, and indeed often where the buoyancy of mind, which is the real curative agent, can be created only by making him wait hopefully for the expected action of medicine; and some physicians still can not unlearn their old training."

"But the change is great. The modern treatment of disease relies very greatly on the so-called natural methods, diet and exercise, bathing and massage; in other words, giving the natural forces the fullest scope by easy and thorough nutrition, increased flow of blood, and removal of obstructions to the excretory systems or to circulation in the tissues."

"One notable example is typhoid fever. At the outset of the nineteenth century it was treated with 'remedies' of the extremist violence--bleeding and blistering, vomiting and purging, antimony and calomel, and other heroic remedies. Now the patient is bathed and nursed and carefully tended, but rarely given medicine."

"This is the result of the remarkable experiments of the Paris and Vienna schools into the action of drugs, which have shaken the stoutest faiths; and partly of the constant and reproachful object lesson of homeopathy. No regular physician would ever admit that the homeopathic 'infinitesimals' could do any good as direct curative agents; and yet it was perfectly certain that homeopaths lost no more of their patients than others. There was but one conclusion to draw, that most drugs had no effect whatever on the diseases for which they were administered."--Ladies Home Journal.

Fire of God

CRITIC

J. C. Allborn writes here, with the intent of discrediting Lake's ministry as well as his person.

July 30, 1924 Editorial in the Spokane Press

LAKE AND THE DOCTORS

Dear Press; In your issue of July 24. Rev. John G. Lake, "divine healer," has called for a showdown from the doctors. He has criticized the medical profession from A to Z. I do not see how he can expect it.

I attended Rev. Dr. Lake's meetings in Spokane for about a year, and did not join his church for that reason. When he said that doctors were liars, damned liars- and further more, experts- that was in a meeting that I attended one Sunday in the Masonic Temple, on Riverside Ave. In January 1919— how can he expect to get a truthful report from them?

I say with all the power of my soul. God bless the doctors. They do the best they know how with the brains God has given them, they work hard and long, spend their time and money for more knowledge to benefit humanity, and if any of us are expecting to find perfection in the medical profession we will never find it, and if we did, all human suffering would be at an end.

I myself am still searching for the truth that Jesus said shall make you free.

I have had an ossified spine now for eight years and have had lots of devils cast out of me. I have been asked to renounce the truth, and if I did not do that would never get my healing, and if I did happen to, it would be the devil that would heal me.

John G. Lake in Spokane   CRITIC

I still believe in the mighty invincible power of God to heal and to sustain life in any living thing, and teach others so. If this is not so, how is it that with an ossified spine, which I believe is the nerve center of the human body, which I have had for eight years, I live, move, and have my being. Yours faithfully.

J. C. Allborn

Fire of God

LAKE ANSWERS ALLBORN

DEAR PRESS: In your issue of July 30 appears a letter from J. C. Allborn of Post Falls, in which he charges that I said: "Doctors were liars, damned liars, and experts." A half truth is the meanest form of a lie. What I actually said was this:

"In the famous Luetgert trial at Chicago, when Luetgert was charged with having reduced his wife to soap and sausage, the medical testimony hinged on whether the bones recovered and introduced as evidence were human or animal bones. The court submitted a mixed assortment of human bones, sheep bones and monkey bones to the medical experts. The doctors were unable to correctly classify the bones. In summing up the evidence the court said: 'Doctors' are divided into three classes, as this expert testimony shows, namely: liars, damned liars, and experts.'"

My writings on this line are in every library. They speak my mind fully. I have no quarrel with honest doctors, but sure have it in for medical grafters. Those who capitalize hopelessness and quit the patient when his money is exhausted.

A recent Spokane case is that of a man with a hopeless paralytic condition--a poor workingman. The doctor demanded $500 to take the case and $50 a month indefinitely. Treatments continued until the patient was totally blind and his money all gone.

I contend this doctor was a scoundrel, and that some legal method of protecting a help-less person from men of this type should be devised; but the honest doctors--God bless them.

John G. Lake in Spokane

Mr. Allborn says he was asked to give up the truth. If it was the same kind of truth that was contained in his letter we would certainly continue to advise him to give it up. Or if he would write a statement of what he believes to be the truth the readers of The Press would be in a better position to judge if he was advised correctly.

JOHN G. LAKE

Fire of God

SPOKESMAN-REVIEW, SPOKANE, WA.
SUNDAY MORNING, JUNE 30, 1918

The Church at Spokane
REV. JOHN G. LAKE, Overseer

Our Reply to All Critics and Inquirers
at Masonic Temple, Sunday, June 23, 1918

We Promised to Present 100 Cases of Healing on Sunday Last.
267 Persons Testified by Standing, to Having Been Healed by the Power of God
32 Persons Gave Public Oral Testimony to the Following Miraculous Cures

Rev. T. Armstrong, a Methodist minister of N 2918 Columbus avenue, healed of a sarcoma growing out of the left shoulder three times as large as a human head.

Rev. Thomas B. O'Riley, 430 Rookery building, healed of fits so violent that it required seven policemen to over power and confine him in the hospital. Instantaneous healing.

Baby Agnes Young, N 169 Post street. Patient at Deaconess hospital for six months for malnutrition: weighed six pounds at birth; at 9 months weighed five pounds. Was removed from hospital; ministered to in prayer; perfectly well in six weeks.

Mrs. Chittenden, Truth church, Coeur d'Alene, Idaho, healed of cancers of the breast.

John G. Lake in Spokane

Mrs. Everetts, 1911 Boone avenue. — Varicose veins; suffered for 38 years; veins enlarged the size of a goose egg; is perfectly healed.

Mrs. Constance Hoag, Puyallup, Wash. — Broke her knee cap and bone protruded through the flesh. Applied an anointed hand-kerchief. Was perfectly healed in an hour. Knee just as well as the other.

Mrs. Walker, Granby Court — Incurable internal cancer; severe case of neuritis; healed through prayer.

Mrs. Harriet Petersen, 2815 Illinois avenue — Was operated on and organs removed. Operated on the second time for gallstones. Bad recovery. Perfectly healed when in state of death. Is now a healthy, normal woman.

Asa Hill, Palouse, Wash. — Rheumatic cripple for 15 years; instantly healed; now works his farm.

Mrs. Wolferman — Injured in G.N.R.R. wreck. Awarded large damages by court. (See court record.) Physicians testified her injuries were such that they destroyed the possibility of motherhood. Healed in answer to prayer. Gave birth to a son at Dr. William T. Penn's private hospital.

Miss Pearl Payne, E 827 Rockwell — Came to Spokane to die. Disease, diabetes, healed, and is working every day.

Miss Jennie Walsh, Union Park, S 116 Fiske street — Gallbladder filled with pus. Physicians insisted on immediate operation. Was instantly healed through prayer.

Fire of God

Mr. Flieshman, Leland, Idaho — Kidney was filled with pus. Physicians said kidney must be removed to save his life. Ministered to and healed when hands were laid upon him.

Mrs. Lamphear, 115 1/2 Sprague avenue — Invalid 11 years. Prolapsus of stomach, bowels of stomach and uterus, tuberculosis and rheumatism. While taking treatments at Soap Lake her left leg grew three inches longer than the other and her foot one inch too long. A bone as large as an orange developed on inside of left knee. Was ministered to at healing rooms. Tubercular lungs healed, leg shortened at the rate of an inch a week, and the bone growth on knee disappeared. Limbs are of equal length. She is perfectly well.

Miss Adelia Koch, 1115 First avenue — Pronounced incurable by 73 physicians (regulars). Later was taken to Osteopathic Institute of Los Angeles. Was a patient there three and a half years. Returned to Spokane in the same dying condition. Had been operated on 26 times. Her father testifies that the doctors got his three houses in Davenport, a valuable wheat ranch of 160 acres, 147 carloads of wood and all the money he had. Is healed and earning her own living.

Mrs. Carter, wife of Policeman Carter, W 31 Pacific avenue — Was examined by seven physicians, who pronounced her condition due to a large fibroid tumor which they estimated would weigh 15 pounds. Was perfectly healed in four ministrations at the healing rooms.

Mrs. O. D. Stutrman, Hansen apartments — Invalid 13 years. Lay in Sacred Heart hospital with a 20 pound weight attached to her foot for 32 days while suffering with inflammatory rheumatism. Begged to be taken home. Preferred to be a cripple rather than endure the torture any

John G. Lake in Spokane

longer. Was instantly healed when Mr. Lake laid his hands upon her and prayed.

Mr. John De Witt of Granby Court — Testified on behalf of his friend, Mr. Fred Narnard, who is 32 years of age. Was injured in babyhood, caused curvature of spine. Was perfectly healed at healing rooms in six days. Height increased one inch. Passed army medical examination and is now in England with troops.

Mr. and Mrs. Harry Lotz stand holding their baby in their arms. Baby developed pus in kidneys and was pronounced incurable by physicians. Instantly healed in answer to prayer.

God in Surgery
Mrs. Gilbertson, N 4115 Helena Street — Hip came out of joint through disease, and would turn like the leg of a doll, showing it was entirely out of socket. Was prayed for at healing rooms while she was suffering in her home, four miles across the city. As prayer was offered the power of God came upon her and the joint was perfectly set.

Remarks by Rev. Lake when testimony was given: Do you hear it, you folks who worship a dead Christ? You doctors, hear it? You preachers, hear it? You doubters, hear it? God set the woman's hip. Because faith in God applied the blessed power to her life.

One of the most remarkable cases in history — The Risdon family stand holding their 6 year old son on their shoulders. This boy was born with a closed head. In consequences the skull was forced upward like the gable of a house, also the forehead was the same. Through the pressure

Fire of God

on the brain the right side became paralyzed and the child could not speak. Under divine healing ministration the bones softened and spread out, the shape of the head became perfectly normal and this paralysis disappeared and he received the power of speech.

Remarks by Rev. Lake — I want you to see that in the spirit of God there is a science far beyond what is termed science and man or woman who enters into spirit relation with God and exercises His power is most scientific.

Mr. Allen, pastor of Pentecostal mission, was dying of pellagra. Was carried from the train into the baggage room as dead. Was instantly healed through the laying on of hands and prayer.

Mrs. Lena Lakey, W 116 Riverside avenue — Instantly healed of violent insanity. An abscess in her left side, from which she had suffered for 15 years disappeared in 24 hours. A heavy rheumatic bone deposit between the bones of the fingers and the joints of the toes disappeared in 48 hours. She is perfectly well.

Mrs. Holder — Healed of insanity while at Medical Lake Institution.

Mrs. Ben Long, 1917 Atlantic street — Instantly healed of paralysis of left side. Her husband, Ben Long was healed of cancer of the stomach. drunkenness and sin. Have established a Godly home and are used in the ministry of healing.

Mrs. John De Witt, Granby Court — Healed of neuritis after years of suffering. Later she was healed when in a state of apparent death following two strokes.

John G. Lake in Spokane

Mrs. Mary Mero, W 717 Nora avenue — Broke her ankle when a child. Suffered for more than fifty years. Was instantly healed.

Mrs. Miles Pearson, E 2815 Illinois avenue — Suffered with a broken ankle a year ago. Improperly set and remained inflamed and swollen as though leg would burst. Healed two weeks ago.

Mrs. Thomas Olsen, Rowan street — Healed when dying of internal cancer. When dying a group of Christian friends gathered about her and prayed. She was instantly healed. Next day walked ten miles. The day following she vomited the entire cancer, body and roots.

Mrs. Richards, Sandpoint, Idaho — Healed when dying of paralysis of one side and internal tumors. The tumors loosened and passed from the body.

Mrs. Allen, Waverly, Wash — A dying, suffering soul from internal cancers. Perfectly healed.

Mrs. Slatter, Harrison, Idaho — Blind nine years. When prayer was offered a vision of Jesus laying His hands upon her eyes appeared to her and she was instantly healed.

Mr. Lake to Audience: All persons here who have been healed by the power of God stand. 267 persons arose.

Fire of God

Gentlemen of the Committee, and Audience, do you see these witnesses? Have you heard the testimonies? Gentlemen of the Committee and Audience, has this been a fair presentation? (Shouts of Yes! Yes! From all parts of the house.)

Did God heal these people? (Cries, Yes! Yes!.)

Is divine healing a fact? (Replies from audience: It surely is.)

Are you entirely satisfied?? (Reply from audience: Indeed, we are)

John G. Lake in Spokane

An Address to the People of the Inland Empire
by John G. Lake, overseer

In the religious life, when one arises with a larger vision of God's purpose for mankind than that usually presented by religious teachers, his declarations are received with question. Men who think desire to be convinced by word, by the Holy Scriptures, and by demonstration, that the teacher's assertions are correct.

It was demanded of the prophets that the signs of a prophet should be seen.

Jesus never intended Christianity to be received and believed on any man's statement, but provided that the statement should be accompanied by an exhibition of spiritual power that would convince the world; saying to His followers:

These signs shall follow them that believe; In my name shall they (the believers) cast out devils; they shall speak with new tongues... they shall lay hands on the sick, and they shall recover.

This was Jesus' own test of truth, also a test of true discipleship.

The people demanded of Jesus: "What sign dost thou show?" They challenged His authority to forgive sins, until convinced by his reasoning and the healing of the palsied man, of His authority and power. Jesus was a reasonable man; He was not only willing to discuss the issue with them, but to heal a man in their presence, as He did, saying:

But that ye may know (be convinced) that the Son of man hath power on earth to forgive sins... I say to you (addressing the palsied man), Arise, take up your bed, and go

Fire of God

to your house; and immediately he rose, took up his bed and went to his house.

> Mark 2:10-12, emphasis Lake's paraphrased

(This was) a mark or brand by which the world might know an imposter and also recognize the true faith of Christ. Christianity was to be its own witness through its power to deliver from sin and heal from disease all who needed deliverance. (See Mark 16:17-18 and John 5:13-15.)

Paul warns Timothy to beware of those who have a form of Godliness but no power of God in their lives, saying:

Having a form of Godliness, but denying the power thereof: from such turn away.

> 2 Timothy 3:5, emphasis Lake's

Paul further declares his own preaching was not based on men's wisdom, but was demonstrated by the power of God through him. He says

And my speech and my preaching was not with enticing words of man's wisdom, but in demonstration of the Spirit and of power: That your faith should not stand in the wisdom of men, but in the power of God.

> 1 Corinthians 2:4-5

When Peter and John healed the lame man at the beautiful gate of the temple, the people demanded, "by what power in what name have ye done this?" And Peter replied:
Be it known unto you all, and to all the people of Israel,

John G. Lake in Spokane

that by the name of Jesus Christ of Nazareth, whom ye crucified, whom God raised from the dead, even by him doth this man stand here before you whole.

> Acts 4:10

Jesus gave a test of the character and quality of the Messenger and the power he exercised. He said, "Ye shall know them by their fruits. Do men gather grapes of thorns or figs of thistles?"

We contend, by the Word of God, that the world and the Church has been robbed of the presence, power, and blessing of Jesus Christ — a present Healer— because the Church has falsely taught that the days of miracles are past. The days of miracles never passed, only in the soul that lost its faith in God. Where faith is, there ever will be the evidence of God's mighty power to save and heal.

The Last Years
in Spokane

The Last years in Spokane

The following pages offer history and memories of Lake's church at Lincoln and Sharp in Spokane, WA. Included are historical accounts of the property as well as personal interviews conducted by the author with those who attended Lake's church.

Big Tabernacle

Tabernacle Erected

      In the early 1920's the Christian Missionary Alliance Organization erected a large rough board shell of a tabernacle at Lincoln and Sharp. This was built as a temporary structure for a convention to be followed by a series of protracted revival services. This enormous structure was built for $3,000.00 with much volunteer labor. It had a dirt floor covered with sawdust and wooden benches. A gigantic furnace in the rear of the building couldn't begin to heat such a wide open place. It was not intended for winter use. It was impossible to keep the place warm in the winter although a wood floor had finally been installed.
      They had intended to tear it down after their series of meetings but several local churches prevailed on them to let it stand so they could rent it from time to time for special meetings.

John G. Lake in Spokane

    In the intervening years many internationally renown evangelists held services there, drawing Pentecostal believers from all over the Inland Empire to the services. Many people are in Heaven today as a result of the moving of the Holy Spirit in that old building. It is still a church today after many remodelings.

Fire of God

Homer and Alice Fritsch remember the Big Tabernacle.

Dr. Lake's church was know as the "Apostolic Tabernacle." It was a long tabernacle type building. Inside there were long wooden benches. For heat in the winter, there was a big wood stove. When it was real cold the people would huddle around it before services. It didn't matter though, because the services were so wonderful.

Alice. This is how a Sunday service was for me. At 1:30 Dr. Lake would have Sunday School. I taught a little boys class. In those days you didn't have separate Sunday School classrooms. There was one class and then a few benches away there would be another class. My little class was down near the piano. You got used to the confusion of many classes. After Sunday School we would have Sunday afternoon service.

The Tabernacle was always just filled. It was very large. There were two rows of benches down the middle and two on the outside of that and they went all the way to the back wall of the church. It would sit close to a thousand people. It was built that way originally because of the large services they were having..

There was a big orchestra. Many young people came to play. One songbook we used was called the Jubilatti, and is now out of print today. It had peppy march time pieces, which just intrigued the young people. We used that as well as the hymnal. Afterwards many stayed after in the back room where they would have potluck. Before they would eat, they would sing "Come and Dine."

Many of the young people would come out to our place on the east end on Friday and Saturday. I would bake a lot of apple pies and cakes.

John G. Lake in Spokane

    My brothers would help Rod Lake clean the church on Saturdays and then would come out to the house. No one was paid in those days. The kids thought it was fun.

    On Sunday nights all the youth would come back for the young peoples meetings. Many played in the orchestra. We were actually in church basically all day on Sundays. That was our life through all those years; to spend time in God's house.

    In a service we would begin by someone coming up and leading the singing. Then they would take prayer requests, and sometimes they would have whole meetings just for testifying. Then John Lake would preach. He would preach for a long time, but it was so good. After he preached then anyone who wanted prayer for healing would come and then they would all go into the prayer room, especially in the evening service. They would pray for hours sometimes. Sometimes we didn't get out of there until eleven or twelve at night. It made a long day, but the people didn't seem to mind. I can't imagine too many people doing that today.

    Another thing they had at the church, were big plays. They were Bible plays. They had dramas. They were highly costumed.

    We have never forgotten the old wood tabernacle. But, the work has gone on by different ones.

Ione Eaton remembers the building and services.

It was a great big, rough structure almost like a barn. The restrooms were on the right side going in. It was an auditorium with no petitions in it. There were many rows of seats.

The building there now is much smaller than Lake's tabernacle. There were wood steps clear across the front of the old building.

It just had a simple frame roof, but it had a real high ceiling. The platform went almost across, except there were instrument rooms on the side. There was another room on the right side that young people gathered in.

The young people's meetings were very special. The anointing was there in the young people's services. Many among the young were ministering.

He never took offerings. There was a little box by the door. People would ask if he was going to take an offering, so once in a while he would mention that if you are so led of the Lord, there is a little box, back there, and if you want to give to the Lord's work, you are welcome to do so. They didn't want to waste their time taking offerings, because they were busy taking care of the needs of the people and worshiping.

He would have home meetings during the week. These meetings were really anointed, they were tremendous. They talked about the Holy Spirit, it was mostly practical teaching.

John G. Lake in Spokane

L. G. Lake remembers:

The church had a large platform and orchestra. It had a wood floor with rows of benches nearly to the back wall.

I remember on many Sundays, my dad would place ads in the Sunday paper with a mini sermon. He had a radio show on KFIO at 12:00 each day.

The orchestra at the church had many instruments including the flute, violin, saxophone, piano, trombone, xylophone.

The building's stove would use 25 cords of wood in the winter time. They would use four foot lengths.

We also had church picnics sometimes. After the Labor day picnic of 1935, my dad had his stroke.

Divine Healing

Dr. Lake's Church
FOURTH AND McCLELLAN

Sunday only, 3 and 8 P. M.

Commencing Monday, Nov. 23d, 7:30

At the Big Tabernacle Every Night

Special Thanksgiving Service Thurs., 3 P. M.

HEAR OUR
GREAT ARAB PREACHER
AND BIBLE STORY TELLER
In NATIVE COSTUME

ABDUL BEN SHINANDAR

ABDUL BEN SHINANDAR
At the Big Tabernacle

LINCOLN AND SHARP   COMMENCING MONDAY 7:30

John G. Lake in Spokane

Abdul Shinandar is John G. Lake
Spokane Daily Chronicle   Nov. 25, 1931

Abdul Ben Shinandar, billed as the "great Christian mystic and Arab story teller," is none other than the Rev. John G. Lake himself.

Appearing "in native costume," Abdul Ben Shinandar has spoken to audiences at the big tabernacle at Lincoln and Sharp this week. Introductions at the evening meeting have been made by B. S. Hebden, local plumber.

The Rev. Mr. Lake has a ready explanation for the fact that no hint of the masquerade appears in the posters and other advertisements of the tabernacle meetings.

Since the advertisements set forth that Abdul Ben Shinandar was companion of Lawrence in Arabia, a Chronicle representative this morning set out to interview the famous Arab.

The Rev. Mr. Lake was reached on the phone. "Is he going to appear at the tabernacle tonight?" Mr. Lake was asked. "I can't say for sure," replied the Rev. Mr. Lake. "You see, he hasn't been going over very well."

Call on Hebden

Mr. Hebden was called. He said he couldn't make arrangements for the interview, but that perhaps Mr. Lake could.

"You see," explained Mr. Hebden, "Abdul Ben Shinandar is Mr. Lake."

The Rev. Mr. Lake later appeared at the Chronicle. He said: "Yes I am Abdul Ben Shinandar. That is the name under which I am registered in the Society of Arab Story Tellers. I am the only Christian missionary ever to be admitted to the society. I qualified in 1911.

Fire of God

"In my early missionary life, I made the acquaintance of W.T. Stead of London, editor of the Review of Reviews, and he financed my trip to Arabia, where I remained a year and seven months."

"I met Lawrence when he was a lieutenant in the British army, long before he came into fame, bringing all the Arabian chiefs together to fight as a common enemy against the Turks in the World war.

Often Lawrence and Adair (an important aide of Lawrence) and I slept under the same blanket."

RADIO LECTURES

Fire of God

John G. Lake was a man who knew how to reach people for Jesus Christ. Whether there were a few or many, he spoke the love of Christ in a way which would uniquely minister to the needs of the group. This continued with John G. Lake embarking upon a relatively new way of reaching the world for Christ. This new ground was the world of radio.

Lake broadcasted at 12 P.M. until 12:15 P.M. on the Spokane radio station KFIO, which broadcasted from a downtown location on the corner of Howard and Riverside.

While only a few of these radio lectures are included in this book, it can be seen by looking into further lectures that it was not uncommon for these lectures to continue as a series in order to teach a whole concept. These lectures were originally compiled and edited by Wilfred Reidt.

John G. Lake in Spokane

Adventures in Religion

Radio Lecture 1

June 24, 1935

This is the first of a series of articles on the general subject of, *"Adventures in Religion."* I want to remind you for a few moments of some of the old mystics who were given glimpses into the unseen that it has not been the privilege of the ordinary man to understand.

The first and foremost was St. Francis of Assisi, whom the world has conceded to be one of the most Christlike characters who has ever lived in the world. At a later period came St. John of the Cross, who for ten years seemed to live detached from the world. Today, he is discovered to be one of the most practical men.

At a later period Madam Guyon appeared on the scene, and most every library contains one of her books. The molding of her character was so amazing that it has caused much discussion in the religious world of our day.

We have only, however, to look over the records of our own land to see many others. Such men as Charles G. Finney, founder of Oberlin College, and its first president. He was a practicing lawyer. He was seized with a conviction for sin so pungent that he returned to the woods to pray, and the Spirit of the Lord came upon him so powerfully, so divinely and took such amazing possession of him, that he tells us he was compelled to cry out to God to cease lest he should die. His wonderful ministry in the land is so well known, his books so frequently found in our libraries, that it is not necessary to discuss him further.

Fire of God

On this list I wish to mention one who is not usually mentioned so lovingly as Finney. He was a Scotch boy, educated in the University of Australia, John Alexander Dowie. In addition to this, the Lord came to him in his own tabernacle one morning as he sat at his desk. Jesus was accompanied by His mother, the Virgin Mary. He advised Dowie concerning his ministry. Jesus laid His hands upon him and from that period his ministry was marked by the supernatural.

It is a matter of public record and one of the most astonishing facts that on one occasion, he invited all persons who were healed under his ministry to attend a meeting at the auditorium in Chicago. Ten thousand people attended the meeting. At the psychological moment they all arose and gave testimony to the fact that they were healed. Those who were not able to attend were asked to send in a card, three and a half inches square, telling of their healing. Five bushel baskets were filled with these cards, representing the testimony of 100,000 people. At the psychological moment these five bushel baskets of cards were spilled over the stage, to emphasize the extent and power of God's ministry and blessing to the people.

Again, I want to call your attention to another marvelous life, that of Hudson Taylor, founder of the China Inland Mission. To him the Lord came, not only in personal presence, but in prophecy concerning the future. It was Hudson Taylor who prophesied the great revival in Wales ten years before it came to pass, giving almost the very day on which it would begin, and its power and extent. All this came to pass just as he had outlined it, while he was in the heart of China.

The Welsh revival was one of the most remarkable revivals that was ever produced. It was apparently prayed out of heaven by a single little church whose lights were never extinguished for seven years. This indicates that if a portion of that congregation was continually in prayer to God, that God

John G. Lake in Spokane

would send a revival. And thus it came, the most astonishing and intensely powerful revival. In small churches which would hold perhaps 500 people, in one corner fifty people would be singing praises of God, thirty-five people would be down praying, another group would be praising God and testifying of His power.

It was not produced by evangelism, but it was the descent of the Spirit of God on the people. Conviction for sin was so powerful, men knelt in their stores or wherever they were to give themselves to God. Sometimes while men were drinking in the public houses at the bar, they would cry out to God and give their hearts to Him.

Beginning with that revival, there was a movement of God that spread throughout the world. In our own land, we were particularly and wonderfully blessed by a movement that began New Year's Eve, 1900, which was accompanied by the Baptism in the Holy Ghost, and multitudes were baptized in the Holy Ghost.

After that revival there arose a phenomenal group of men and women. I am going to mention a few. The first I am going to mention is Aimee Semple McPherson. She was a young girl on a farm in Ontario, Canada. She attended a meeting by a young Irishman, Robert Semple, who was preaching under the anointing of the Holy Ghost. She became convicted of sin, opened her heart to God and found Him, and was baptized in the Holy Ghost. Finally they were married and went as missionaries to China, where he died of fever. She was left a widow, and soon with a newborn baby. Some friends provided the funds that brought her back to the United States.

Later she formed the acquaintance of a fine young businessman, and decided to settle down and forget all her burning call to the Gospel. This she tried to do. Two children were born to them. And then one day God came to Aimee in a meeting at Berlin, Ontario, conducted by Rev. Hall. Her early

Fire of God

ministry, for a period of about fifteen years surpassed everything that we have ever seen in any land since the days of the apostles. (A multitude was healed under her ministry.)

Again, I want to call your attention to another unusual man, Raymond Ritchie, who belonged to Zion, Illinois. His father was mayor of Zion City at one time. This boy was tubercular. They did not seem to understand his difficulty. He had no ambition; he could not work like other boys. He was in a state of lassitude. Eventually he found God. We speak of finding God as the old Methodist Church spoke of being saved, getting religion, meaning one and the same thing. When a man confesses his sin and God comes into his heart and gives him the peace and consciousness of his salvation, he has found God.

Young Ritchie, after his salvation, was so absorbed in prayer, and the family got sort of worried. The father finally told him he had to get to work and help earn his living. But some woman who understood the boy said, "I have a room you can have." Another said she would provide him with food to keep him alive.

The great war came on, and the epidemic of the flu followed, when men died by the thousands throughout this United States. He became stirred and began to pray for people and they were healed. The medical department presently took notice of it, and they sent him to pray for sick soldiers, and they were healed. Very well, he has continued in the ministry from then until now, and some of the most wonderful healing meetings that have ever taken place, he has conducted.

Another man God has marvelously blessed and used is Dr. Price. He belongs to our own locality. Price used to live in Spokane. Dr. Price was baptized in the Spirit. Right away he began to manifest a most amazing ministry of healing. I attended one of his meetings at Vancouver, B.C. He had four audiences a day and 15,000 people in each, and people for a

John G. Lake in Spokane

block around who could not get inside. All the churches in Vancouver, I think, united with him in that meeting. It was the most amazing meeting I ever saw. The sick people stood in groups of fifty and he would anoint them with oil according to the fifth chapter of James, and then pray for them. They were so overpowered by the Spirit they would fall to the floor, and a great number were healed.

Radio Lecture 2

June 25, 1935

No greater book has ever been given to mankind than the Bible. The amazing things recorded there that men experienced and that men wrought in the Name of Jesus Christ though faith, by power of God stand forever as an incentive to every man who enters and labors where they did. There is a place in God into which the soul enters a relationship to God that leaves the registry of heaven here in your heart and that makes it possible for the Spirit of God through you as His agent, to register in the hearts of others.

Harry Fosdick says, "Until the new theology can produce the sinless character of the old theology, it stands challenged." We believe that. We believe that the old-fashioned salvation through the blood of Jesus Christ and the Baptism of the Holy Ghost make possible an experience that no other religious experience in the world has ever been able to produce.

In the year 1900, there came a new wave of heavenly experience to this land and to the world. It began in Topeka, Kansas. It was in a Bible School conducted by Charles Parham. The founding of that school was an amazing thing. He was moved of God to go to Topeka, Kansas. He obeyed the prompting of the Spirit and went to the city. After looking all around for a building suitable for a Bible School and finding none, one day a gentleman told him of a residence on the outskirts of the city. It contained about twenty-two or more rooms, and it was unoccupied. The owner lived in California. He went to see the building, and as he stood looking at it the Spirit of the Lord said, "I will give you this building for your Bible School." And he said to himself, "This is the house."

John G. Lake in Spokane

As he stood there a gentleman came up to him and said "What about the house?" Parham told him what the Lord had said to him, and the man, being the owner of the house said, "If you want to use this building for a Bible School for God it is yours," and he handed him the key without any more ado.

The next day he went to the train and met a young woman of his acquaintance. She told him that when she was praying, the Spirit of God told her there was going to be a Bible School here and that she should come. She was the first student. Thirty-five students came, all correspondingly directed by the Spirit of God.

This group began a study of the Word of God to discover what really constituted the Baptism of the Holy Ghost. After a month of study they became convinced that there was one peculiarity that accompanied the Baptism of the Holy Ghost--speaking in tongues.

They went to seeking the Baptism of the Holy Ghost. Parham was not present at the time. On New Year's night at twelve o'clock, 1900, one of the group, a Miss Osmand, a returned missionary was baptized in the Holy Ghost and began to speak in tongues. In a few days the entire group, with a couple of exceptions, was baptized in the Spirit. When Parham returned and found that the students in his school had been baptized in the Holy Ghost, he himself went down before the Lord, and God baptized him in the Holy Ghost, too.

I want you to keep this story in mind for it forms the basis of the wonderful experience I want to relate in my next talk.

Fire of God

Radio Lecture 3

June 26, 1935

For a moment I want to call attention to a challenge that has been distributed widely through the ministry of Henry Fosdick, as I mentioned yesterday. Fosdick has said, "Until the new theology can produce the sinless character of the old theology, it (the new theology) stands challenged."

That is our position. We are reminding you, friends, that God is a miracle God. God is a miracle. Jesus Christ is a miracle. His birth was a miracle. His life was a miracle. His death was a miracle. His resurrection from the grave was a miracle. His Ascension was a miracle. His reception at the Throne of God by the eternal Father was the greatest of all miracles. Because of that God then gave Him the gift of the Holy Ghost, and made Him the administrator of the Spirit forever.

Some things can be better taught by relating experiences than in any other way. I might try to impress you with the beauty and wonder of the Baptism of the Holy Ghost, but dear friends, I think the relating of a few experiences will make it clearer to our minds than any other way.

I am reminded of an incident that took place on a railway train. Father Neiswender was stricken with a paralytic stroke. He had not been able to sleep for weeks. When they got him on a train to bring him to Spokane, the motion of the train temporarily soothed him and he fell asleep and dreamed. In his dream an angel came to him and said, "When you get to Spokane, inquire for a man by the name of Lake. He will pray for you and God will heal you." He was directed to our place, and when we prayed for him he immediately began to use his paralyzed arm and side, but was not completely delivered. The third time I went to pray the Lord showed me a blood clot in the

John G. Lake in Spokane

spinal cord as large as a bead. I prayed until the blood clot disappeared. No one could explain an incident like that by any natural law. Consequently, we must classify it in the line of miracles IN OUR DAY--not a thousand years ago

One more incident of this order: A family by the name of Bashor had a lovely boy who became dissatisfied at home and ran away. He went to a farmer where he was not known, gave another name, and worked for him a year. In the meantime the family, with the aid of the police searched everywhere for the boy, but he could not be found. One day the mother came to me brokenhearted and told me the story. We knelt and prayed and asked God that He would cause that boy to get in touch with his parents.

Two days later she received a letter from the boy. He told her that on the night we had prayed he went to bed and had an unusual vision. Jesus appeared and talked to him. Jesus said;

I forgive your sins, but I want you to write to your mother, and get home to your folks.

The boy was greatly moved, got up and told the farmer the incident, and the result was the farmer hitched up his team and brought the boy in to his home. That boy is now married and has a nice family, and still lives in Spokane.

The part of that incident that might interest young folks is this. I was preaching at Mica, Washington, where I related this incident. A young lady in the audience listened to the story, and after the meeting she said to me, "I would like to get acquainted with that young man." She did, and he is her husband.

Dear friends, these are some of the things that show us that there is a work of God's Spirit different from what we are ordinarily accustomed to, and these are the things that make religion real to New Testament Christians. Different ones in the scriptures were guided by dreams. Joseph was guided by dreams. Some were guided by a voice from heaven. Now we are contending and bringing to your attention that there was an experience provided by the Lord Himself that made that intimacy a possibility. That is, the Baptism of the Holy Spirit. I wish I might say that with such emphasis that it would penetrate the deep recesses of your spirit.

One more incident. Over in the woods back of Kellogg, Idaho, lived a family by the name of Hunt. I visited in their home just a little while ago. The aged father was given up to die, the son was very anxious about him. The father kept saying, "Son, I ought not to die." The son had been much in prayer about this matter. One day he stood on a log road and presently he said a man appeared a little distance ahead, and as the gentleman approached he addressed Mr. Hunt saying, "I am Mr. Lake. I have Healing Rooms in Spokane. If you will bring your father there, the Lord will heal him." He was so impressed, that he got his father and brought him to me for prayer, and the Lord healed him gloriously and he lived many years.

Dr. John G. Lake, 1916

The value of the ministry of healing is not in the mere fact that people are healed. The value of healing is more largely the fact that it becomes a demonstration of the living, inner, vital power of God, which should dwell in every life and make us new and mighty men in the hands of God.

John G. Lake in Spokane

Radio Lecture 4

June 27, 1935

When the German army started their famous march on Belgium and France with an army of three million men, they came to the borders only to find that they were met with such a tremendous opposition that for ten full days they were compelled to stay back until they could bring up their heavy artillery. Statesmen of Germany declare that, the ten days' delay resulted in their losing the war. France and Belgium were prepared in the meantime to meet the assault.

Jesus Christ, the Son of God, said to His disciples:

"Behold, I send you forth as sheep (in the midst of) wolves" (Luke 10:3)

but He did not send them out without being prepared. They were commissioned and empowered by God, for that is what constitutes the Baptism of the Holy Ghost. Jesus Christ gave His disciples a big program before He left them. He told them they were not only to preach the Gospel to the whole world, but that they were to demonstrate its power.

Go ye into all the world, and preach the gospel to every creature...And these
signs shall follow them that believe; In my name shall they cast out devils;
they shall speak with new tongues; They shall take up serpents; and if they
drink any deadly thing, it shall not hurt them; they shall lay hands on the sick,
and shall recover (Mark 16:15-18).

Fire of God

These signs shall follow them that believe--those who accepted their work.

Dear friends, men who were going to put a program like that into effect needed heavy artillery from heaven. That is what Jesus undertook to give from heaven. So He said they were not to go out right away unprepared. Instead He said:

"Tarry ye in the city of Jerusalem, until ye be endued with power from on high" (Luke 24:49).

That endowment from on high is the equipment of every child of God who follows the biblical pattern. We are trying to impress upon the minds of men that one of the greatest adventures in religion that this world ever has found was when men dared to step across the usual boundaries and dared receive from His hand the Baptism of the Holy Ghost, which equips them with the power of God to bring blessings to other lives.

Just for one moment I want to bring you this fact. That the first thing Jesus said would be manifested in the Christian's life the first thing in Christian experience, and the exercise of Christian power that Jesus said would follow the Christian's life. They had power to cast out devils.

Jesus first gave that power to twelve, then He gave it to the seventy, then He gave it to the Church at large on the Day of Pentecost, when the Baptism of the Holy Ghost descended upon 120 at Jerusalem. Jesus gave the equipment from heaven.

In our day, within the past thirty years, we have seen such a manifestation of God from heaven as no other century in the world's history ever saw with the exception of the first four centuries of the Christian era. Beginning with 1900, the Spirit of God began to be poured out in power upon the world so that every country in the world has received this amazing power of God. Men who were ordinary businessmen, men who were scholars and teachers, students, and men from every walk in life

John G. Lake in Spokane

found this equipment from heaven by the grace of God, and stepped out into a great life and ministry for God. This preparation, friends, is not for preachers only, but for the people. Jesus said,

"These signs shall follow them that BELIEVE" (Mark 16:17).

Friends, there is an adventure for your soul, the most amazing adventure in all the world. It takes a brave soul to set into the light of God and receive the equipment He provides. That is no place for a coward. A cowardly spirit, a spirit that is always hiding always apologizing for his faith, will never enter there. That is the gate of God. That is the gate into His Spirit. That is the gate into a life of effectiveness for every one who wants to serve God aright. Friends, you need this equipment to meet the demands of this day.

Sanctification is the cleansing of a man's nature by the indwelling power of the Spirit of Christ, for the purpose of the transformation of the mind and nature of man into the mind and nature of Jesus Christ.

I like John Wesley's definition of sanctification: "Possessing the mind of Christ, and ALL the mind of Christ."

Fire of God

Radio Lecture 5

June 28, 1935

This afternoon I want to talk to you on the subject of Miracles. From the year 400 until now the Church has assumed the attitude that the days of miracles are passed without any scriptural evidence whatever. They have taught that miracles were to demonstrate the divinity of Jesus, and therefore, the divinity of Jesus being demonstrated there was no longer any need for miracles.

We had a local incident that demonstrates the effect of this teaching I think. My convictions on the matter is that it has done more damage to the Christian faith than any other teaching that has been promulgated. There is a gentleman who works at the Davenport Hotel in Spokane, O. A. Risdon, who is one of the engineers there. He had a son with a deformed head. The top of the head raised up like the ridge of a roof, the forehead and back of the head also were forced out into similar manner, giving the head the appearance of the hull of a yacht upside down. He was born with what the physicians call a closed head. The boy was always slobbering; the pressure on the brain caused the right side to become paralyzed, and the boy was dumb. He was five years old at this time.

The physicians said there was nothing they could do. Then in desperation he appealed to his pastor. The pastor told him the days of miracles were past; that the Lord did not heal now; that miracles were given to demonstrate the divinity of Jesus. The father replied, "If Jesus would heal my son, I would be convinced that He is divine now. If He is divine, He would lift this damnation from our house."

Finally, he came to us seeking help. We began to minister to the child. In a few days we observed that the

John G. Lake in Spokane

paralysis began to depart; instead of walking on one side of his ankles he began to walk on the foot, and that indicated that the pressure was relieved on the brain. In seven weeks the child was perfectly well. The bones of the head softened and came down to normal. The paralysis disappeared and the child began to talk. In three months he was in the public school. He is a young married man now.

Dear friends, if we had continued to believe that the days of miracles were past that boy would be in the insane asylum. But we believed that Jesus Christ was the same yesterday, today and forever, and the boy was healed. It is a delight to believe the *Words of Jesus*. I have used this rule in my study of the Scriptures. If there is any question on any scripture I settle it with the *Words of Jesus*. I consider all the scriptures are a common court of the Gospel, but the Words of Jesus are the supreme court of the Gospel. When I want a supreme court decision, I appeal to the Words of Jesus.

You can read all the Words of Jesus in two hours or less in a Red Letter New Testament. Make a practice of reading the Words of Jesus on any subject that troubles you, and make a compilation of what He says. He ought to be sufficient authority on any question for the heavenly Father called attention to the fact that He is the Son of God, and that we are to hear Him. He said:

"This is my beloved Son, in whom I am well pleased; hear ye him" *(*Matthew 17:5).

Fire of God

Radio Lecture 6

July 2, 1935

Jesus Christ came on the scene as a challenger. We have almost come to believe in our day that He was a sentimentalist and an easy type. He was King. He was the Prince of God. He was the Glory of Heaven! He was the representative of the Eternal Father! He had a mission. He declared the Father. He stepped among the religions of the earth as the challenger.

Jesus said there was real sin, that there was real sickness, that there was real death. He was not dodging the issue. He met it foursquare, and He said, I am bigger than it all. I am the Prince of Life. He destroyed sin and obliterated it from the souls of men. He blasted sickness and dissolved it from their system. He raised the dead to life. He challenged the devil, who was the author of death, to destroy Him if he could. He went into the regions of death and conquered and came forth triumphant so that it became necessary for the Lord to have a new vocabulary. He said after coming forth from the grave,

"All power is given unto me in heaven and in earth. Go ye therefore, and teach all nations, baptizing them in the name of the Father, and of the Son, and of the Holy Ghost" (Matthew 28:18-19).

Sin and sickness and death, the triumvirate of darkness, that Jesus met and overcame were the original forces of evil in the world--the manifestation of the kingdom of darkness. There never will be a heaven, there never could be one, where these exist. Their destruction is necessary. Jesus realized that. He came to do what man could not do for himself. That is one of the reasons why men cannot save themselves. All the good works that man may perform from now to the day of his death will not save him. Sin is of the heart. It is in the nature. Jesus came to reconstruct man's nature and give him instead of his own evil nature, the nature of God. Sin has made the nature of man vile. Christ came to give him deliverance from this nature and give him a new nature, the divine nature.

Through sin death entered into the world (see Romans 5:12).

Death is not a servant of God, nor a child of God, nor a product of God. Sin is the ENEMY of God. The New Testament declares that

"The last enemy that shall be destroyed is death" (1 Corinthians 15:26).

Not the last servant or friend, but the last enemy. Death is doomed to destruction by the Lord Jesus Christ. Sin and sickness are incipient death.

That is the reason we do not speak of the things of the Lord and His salvation in moderate tones. We are shouting them to mankind. The spirit of a real child of God challenges darkness, challenges sin, challenges sickness. The Lord Jesus came to destroy sickness and wipe it out of the lives of men, to make possible the heaven of God in their hearts and lives now. There could be no heaven where disease and sickness are found. Sin and sickness and death must be blotted out. That is the reason, dear friends, that Christianity is always a challenger. Christianity is a thing of strength. Real religion is a source of power. It is the dynamite of God. The Holy Spirit gives the overcoming grace and strength essential to destroy sin, to destroy sickness, to overcome death.

Fire of God

Radio Lecture 7

July 3, 1935

I am pleased to greet you today, dear friends, with a real account of one of the marvelous adventures in God. Jesus said,

"Heal the sick, cleanse the lepers, raise the dead, cast out devils; freely ye have received, freely give." (Matthew 10:8).

Christianity was not to be stinted in her giving. She was not to be a beggar. She was to be a giver. She had something from heaven to give that the world did not have. She had something to give that would bring deliverance to the world. Jesus was putting His program of deliverance in force through the Church.

The man is a bold man who undertakes to carry out this program of Jesus. The Christian who never has faith enough in God to undertake it, I fear, is of the cowardly type. I am afraid that modern Christianity stands indicted at the bar of God for cowardliness because of fear to undertake the program of Jesus.

Friends, that is why we urge upon men the necessity of the Baptism of the Holy Ghost. It is the only thing that brings the heavenly equipment to the hearts of men, that makes them equal to this program and the possibility of carrying it out.

I want to talk to you today of a bold soul, and in my judgement a very extraordinary one indeed. I refer to a gentleman who lives in this city, a preacher of the gospel from the days of his youth, Rev. C. W. Westwood. His home is on Nora Avenue.

A number of years ago there was born at one of the great hospitals of the city a little child (a girl) from healthy parents, Mr. and Mrs. Young. Mr. Young for many years had

John G. Lake in Spokane

a stall in the Westlake Market. Mrs. Young has been a nurse for many years and also is well known. When this baby was born it weighed six and a half pounds. Because of some strange difficulty the child could not assimilate its food. When she was nine months old she only weighed four and a half pounds. The child looked more like a little dried up alligator than it did like a human being. She finally fell into a state of death and remained in a dying condition. In the meantime, we were called to minister to the child.

Mr. Westwood was assigned to the case. One day when he went to the hospital as usual to minister to the child, they explained that the child was not there. It had died that morning and was in the dead room. He asked if he might see the child, and went into the dead room, and took the child down. He sat down on a chair with the baby on his knees. He opened his heart to God, turned the spirit of faith in his heart loose in behalf of the little one. In a little while (and I am saying this with all reverence before God, because I expect to meet this matter when I stand before the great Judgment Throne), the child revived. He sent for the parents, they took the child from the hospital and put her in the hands of an elderly lady by the name of Mrs. Mason, who nursed her for six weeks. At the end of that period she was as well as any other child. Her name is Agnes Young.

About a year ago I received a telephone call from Agnes Young asking me if I would perform a marriage ceremony for her and her fiancee. This young couple lives at Eugene, Oregon, now.

And so I want to leave this testimony, that God is as good as His Word. That faith in Almighty God brings to pass the very same things today that it always did.

Fire of God

Radio Lecture 8

July 5, 1935

The climax of all adventures was the adventure of Jesus in delivering men from sin and sickness and death. One cannot measure the Man of Galilee with any tapeline or yardstick that comes from human reasoning. Jesus is outside of the realm of reason. In the first place, His history was written by the prophets, ages before He was born. Man can write a better history of Jesus from the Old Testament than they can from the New Testament. In the New Testament we have simply a little fragment about His incarnation and birth and then thirty years of silence, except for a little glimpse of Him when He was twelve years of age. All the books that have been written of Jesus have been written almost entirely about His three years of public ministry that began with His baptism in the Jordan and closed with His resurrection. Now men try to write on His pre-existence. Here and there one has caught a glimpse of His ministry, seated at the right hand of the Majesty on High.

I want you to see another fact, that every prophecy that was written before His time was all in the miracle realm. His incarnation was a real miracle. He was not born under the natural laws of generation. He was conceived of the Holy Ghost. He was a true incarnation--God uniting Himself with humanity. The scenes surrounding His birth--the angelic visitation, the coming of the wise men were all miracles. The angel's warning to Joseph to flee with the child to Egypt was miraculous. The very silence of those thirty years is considered most miraculous. The divine silences represent the most marvelous elements in the Book we all love. The descent of the Spirit at His baptism was a miracle. From that day until Mount Olivet was a period of miracles. His life among men was a miracle. The new kind of life that He revealed to the world was a miracle. Jesus' mental processes were miraculous. Our libraries are full of books written by great thinkers, like Thomas Edison, and others, who were incessant thinkers. With Jesus there is something different. He speaks out from the Spirit that dominated His spiritual faculties. Jesus' spirit ruled His intellect. Gems of divine truth dripped from His lips as honey from the honeycomb. The sermon on the Mount and great portions in Luke and John are as untouched as when they dropped from the lips of Jesus. Men's writings grow old and out of date. God's truth is ever fresh. Yes, Jesus' words and life and contact with men was miraculous; It is still miraculous.

His death on the cross, His days in the tomb, His dramatic and startling resurrection, were all miracles. His presence among the disciples on different occasions and finally his ascension in the presence of 500 witnesses, were miracles. They do not belong to the reason realm— they belong to the miracle realm. Jesus was in the realm of the Spirit, the realm of faith, the realm where God acts, the realm where the real child of God lives. You see, Christians have been translated out of the realm of human thought and reason into the kingdom of the Son of His love, the realm of the Spirit.

It would be uncharitable if we were to criticize the man of reason, who knows nothing about the spiritual realm. Christianity is not the product of human reasoning. Christianity is a divine intervention. Christians are those who have been 'born from above." They have been recreated. This life of God that comes into their spirit nature, dominates the reason so that they have the "mind of Christ" to think God's thoughts and live in God's realm of miracles.

Friends, when a Christian tries to live by REASON he is moving out of God's country into the enemy's land. We belong in the miraculous or supernatural realm.

Fire of God

Christ was a miracle. Every Christian is a miracle. Every answer to prayer is a miracle. Every divine illumination is a miracle. The power of Christianity in the world is a miraculous power. God help us to realize that ours is a High and Holy Calling.

Hymn No. 70

FATHER FABER'S WONDERFUL HYMN
"Souls of Men, Why Will Ye Scatter?"

"We all like sheep have gone astray."—Isa. 53:6.

1.
Souls of men, why will ye scatter
Like a crowd of frightened sheep?
Foolish hearts! why will ye wander
From a love so true and deep?
Was there ever kinder Shepherd,
Half so gentle, half so sweet,
As the Savior who would have us
Come and gather round his feet?

2.
It is God! his love looks mighty,
But is mightier than it seems;
'Tis our Father, and His fondness
Goes far out beyond our dreams.
There's a wideness in God's mercy,
Like the wideness of the sea;
There's a kindness in His justice,
Which is more than liberty.

3.
There is no place where earth's sorrows
Are more felt than up in heaven;
There is no place where earth's failings

Have such kindly judgment given.
There is welcome for the sinner,
And more graces for the good;
There is mercy with the Savior;
There is healing in His blood.

4.
But we make His love too narrow,
By false limits of our own;
And we magnify His strictness
With a zeal He will not own.
There is plentiful redemption
In the blood that has been shed;
There is joy for all the members
In the sorrows of the Head.

5.
If our love were but more simple,
We should take Him at His word;
And our lives would all be sunshine
In the sweetness of our Lord.
For the love of God is broader
Than the measures of man's mind;
And the heart of the Eternal
Is most wonderfully kind.

John G. Lake in Spokane

Radio Lecture 9

July 9, 1935

I want to talk to you concerning some of the purposes of God. Among them is God's amazing purpose to baptize men in the Holy Spirit. I think that even among the deepest Christians in our day little is understood of the real purpose of God in this wonderful experience.

We say to one another that the Baptism of the Holy Spirit is God coming into man; that it is God manifesting Himself in man, and other expressions of this type, but it fails to convey to the mind anything like the great purpose of God in His incoming in us.

The Baptism of the Holy Spirit has among its wonderful purposes the dwelling of God in us, the perfecting of His life in us through His Word in our spirit, through His power in our life. Tongues is the peculiar manifestation of God accompanying the coming of God the Holy Spirit into our life. This was the evidence when the Holy Spirit of God descended on the Day of Pentecost at Jerusalem. The Scripture is given in these wonderful words:

> Suddenly there came a sound from heaven as of a rushing mighty wind, and it
> filled all the house where they were sitting. And there appeared unto them
> cloven tongues like as of fire, and it sat upon each of them. And they were all
> filled with the Holy Ghost, and began to speak with other tongues, as the Spirit
> gave them utterance (Acts 2:2-4).

Fire of God

What is the real purpose? What is God doing? Is He giving to the individual certain powers to demonstrate and to convince the world? I do not think that is the real reason. There is a deeper one. God is taking possession of the inner spirit of man. From the day that Adam sinned the spirit of man was a prisoner. This prison condition continues until God releases the spirit of the individual in the Baptism of the Holy Ghost. The spirit remains dumb, unable to express itself to mankind, until God through the Holy Ghost releases the spirit, and the voice of the spirit is restored.

You understand man is a triune being; spirit, soul and body, and these departments of our life are very different. God manifests Himself to the spirit of man; and the experience of real salvation is the coming of God into the spirit of man and the infusion of the spirit of man and God.

In the olden days the Church used to discuss the subject of sanctification but was somewhat hazy in its explanation of what it was. Sanctification is God taking possession of our mental forces, just as He took possession of our spirit when He bestowed on us eternal life. Your mind is brought into harmony with God even as your spirit was brought into harmony with God. Following the example of Jesus we dedicate not only our spirit and soul (or mind) to God, but also our body to God. That is the reason we left doctors and medicine behind.

I want to talk to you about speaking in tongues by relating this experience, and reciting a poem God gave me, when I was a missionary in South Africa and had my residence there. There was a dreadful epidemic of African Fever and within thirty days about one-fourth of the population of some sections of the country of both white and black died. I was absent from my tabernacle on the field with a group of missionaries and we did the best we could to get them healed of God, and help bury the dead. I returned to my tabernacle

John G. Lake in Spokane

after about three weeks' absence to discover that the same thing was taking place there. I was greatly distressed. My pianist was gone; my chief soloist was gone--the only daughter of an aged mother. I went to her home to console her and comfort her. As I sat by her table she reminded me that just four weeks before I had been present when the pianist and the soloist were practicing music in that home. My soul was very sorrowful. As I sat meditating I began to pray: "My God, I would like to know what sort of reception such a soul as that gets when they arrive on the other side. Presently God spoke to my soul and said, "Take your pen and I will tell you about it."

The first thing that came was the name of the poem in tongues. Then the Lord gave me the interpretation. It was called "The Reception." Then the first verse came in tongues, then I received from the Lord the interpretation, and then the next verses likewise, and so on. In the meantime something transpired in my own spirit. I felt as if I was being elevated into the presence of God, and I could look down on the folks on earth and it was described in these verses:

The Reception

List! 'Tis the morning hours in Glory.
A shadow through the mists doth now appear.
A troop of angels sweeping down in greeting.
A "Welcome Home" rings out with joyous cheer.

A traveler from the earth is now arriving,
A mighty welcome's ringing in the skies!
The trumpets of a host are now resounding,
A welcome to the life that never dies.

Who is the victor whom the angels welcome?
What mighty deeds of valor have been done?

Fire of God

What is the meaning of these shouts of triumph?
Why welcome this soul as a mighty one?

She's but a woman, frail and slight and tender,
No special mark of dignity she bears,
Only the Christ light from her face doth glisten,
Only the white robe of a saint she wears.

She's but a soul redeemed through the blood of Jesus.
Hers but a life of sacrifice and care;
Yet with her welcome all the heaven's ringing,
And on her brow a victor's crown she bears.

How come she thus from sin's benighting thraldom,
The grace and purity of heaven to obtain?
Only through Him Who gave His life a ransom,
Cleansing the soul from every spot and stain.

See! As you gaze upon her face so radiant,
'Tis but the beauty of her Lord you see,
Only the image of His life resplendent,
Only the mirror of His life is she.

See with what signs of joy they bear her onward,
How that the heavens ring with glad acclaim!
What is the shout they raise while soaring upward?
"Welcome! Thrice welcome, thou, in Jesus' Name!"

Rest in the mansion by the Lord prepared thee,
Out of the loving deeds which thou has done,
Furnished through by thoughts and acts which have
portrayed Me,
Unto a lost world as their Christ alone.

John G. Lake in Spokane

Hear how thy heavenly harp is ringing!
Touched are its strings with hands by thee unseen.
Note that the music of thine own creating,
Heaven's melodies in hearts where sin has been.

See how the atmosphere with love is laden,
And that with brightness all landscape gleams!
Know 'tis the gladness and the joy of heaven
Shed now by rescued souls in radiant beams.

Oh, that here on earth we may learn the lesson
That Christ enthroned on our hearts while here,
Fits and prepares the soul for heaven,
Making us like Him both there and here.

Doing the simple and homely duties
Just as our Christ on the earth has done,
Seeking alone that the Christ's own beauty
In every heart should be caused to bloom.

Showing all men that the blood of Jesus
Cleanses our hearts from all sin below,
And that the life of the Christ within us
Transforms the soul till as pure as snow.

When we thus come to the dark cold river,
No night, no darkness, no death is there,
Only great joy that at last the Giver,
Grants us anew of His life to share.

Given to John G. Lake
in Tongues and Interpretation while in Africa

Fire of God

Radio Lecture 10

July 10, 1935

Today I want to talk to you concerning one of the remarkable and outstanding incidents in the Word of God. You will find it in Acts 19:11-12. It reads:

"And God wrought special miracles by the hands of Paul: So that from his body were brought unto the sick handkerchiefs or aprons, and the diseases departed from them, and the evil spirits went out of them."

The people brought their handkerchiefs or aprons to the Apostle Paul that they might touch his person. They were then carried to the sick and laid on them; the demons went out of them and the sick were healed.

An examination of this incident discloses one of the most wonderful facts I know. First, that the Spirit of God is tangible. We think of the air as tangible, of electricity as tangible and we register the effects of it. And I want to say to you, friends, that the Spirit of God is equally as tangible and can be handled and distributed--It can be enclosed in handkerchief or apron and sent as a blessing to the one who needs it.

Get this scripture and read it for yourself and secure from heaven the blessing it contains, and remember when you are in a struggle and doubts and fears assail you, that God is not far away in the heavens. His Spirit is right here to bless, here to act in your life for a blessing.

Along with this line I want to present this testimony of Mrs. Constance Hoag, who is dean of women at the state college, Pullman, Washington. She was visiting her son at

John G. Lake in Spokane

Fairfield, Washington. They were going for a motor ride. When she stepped on the running board, her son thinking she was already in the car, started the car. She fell and broke the kneecap and the bone protruded through the flesh. They carried her into the house, then called us on the long distance and asked that we pray and send her a handkerchief as soon as possible by messenger. We sent the handkerchief and in fifteen minutes after she received it the bone had gone back into place. In forty-five minutes the knee was entirely well.

However, her friends began to challenge this healing and she found herself in the midst of a strange debate. A little later almost the same accident happened again. She was thrown to the pavement and the other kneecap was broken and protruded in two sections through the flesh. Once again we prayed over a handkerchief and sent it to her, and once again the power of God acted, but this time not so quickly as the first time. The second time she said the pain was gone in half an hour; in a hour the bone had gone back in its place and in a hour and a half the knee was healed and she was well. Friends the Spirit of God is tangible today as it was in the days of the Apostle Paul.

Fire of God

Radio Lecture 11

July 11, 1935

This morning I was out on the extreme east side of the city. I ran across a strange thing. A man was coming down the street with a pack on his back. The pack was in a cowhide which was only about half cured. In the sack he had a cow's leg. As I came up to him he said, "Excuse me, sir, but this is my Christian cross."

I said, "Excuse me, but it looks like just the opposite to me." He went down the street and as far as I could hear him he was scolding me.

Then I went to the home of a woman who had been ill a long time. She had lain in bed and was gradually growing worse, and all the time she was accepting this sickness as from God. So I told her this foolish incident and I said, "Dear woman, if you knew the Word of God you would never accept a thing like that as the will of God, because Jesus most emphatically declared that sickness was not the will of God but the devil's."

She had accepted that rotten, nasty business as God's will and had lain in bed for eight months. It is as offensive to God as the man with his "Christian cross." I want you to know, dear friends, that the Word of God is the foundation upon which our faith is to be built.

Jesus said that He came, *"to destroy the works of the devil."*

John G. Lake in Spokane

Acts 10:38 declares:

"How God anointed Jesus of Nazareth with the Holy Ghost and with power: who went about doing good, and healing all that were OPPRESSED OF THE DEVIL; for God was with him."

You do not find "if it be Thy will" in the teaching of Jesus. He never suggested in word or deed that sin, sickness and death were the will of God. The leper who came to Jesus for healing in the eighth (chapter) of Matthew did say;

"Lord, if thou wilt, thou canst make me clean."

I suppose he, too, was accepting the dirty leprosy as the will of God.
Jesus instantly said,

"I will; be thou clean."

The answer of Jesus to the leper is Jesus' answer to you, to every sick man. "If it be thy will" was never suggested in any of Jesus' teaching concerning sickness and disease. Friend, Jesus had declared His will in the most emphatic manner. His will is always to heal if you but come to Him.

Dr. John G. Lake, 1909

Every student of the primitive Church discerns at once a distinction between the soul of the primitive Christian and the soul of the modern Christian. It lies in the spirit of Christ's dominion.

Fire of God

The Holy Spirit came into the primitive Christian soul to elevate his consciousness in Christ, to make him greater. He smote sin, and it disappeared. He cast out devils (demons); a divine flash from his nature overpowered and cast out the demon. He laid his hands on the sick, and the mighty Spirit of Jesus Christ flamed into the body and the disease was annihilated. He was commanded to rebuke the devil, and the devil would flee from him. He was a reigning sovereign, not shrinking in fear, but overcoming by faith.

It is this spirit of DOMINION, when restored to the Church of Christ, that will bring again the glory-triumph to the Church of God throughout the world and lift her into the place where, instead of being the obedient servant of the world, the flesh and the devil, she will become the divine instrument of God. She will minister Christ's power and salvation in healing the sick, in the casting out of demons, and in the carrying out of the whole program of Jesus' ministry as the early Church did.

John G. Lake in Spokane

Radio Lecture 12

August 22, 1935

I want to tell you the story of an unusual family. I am going to call this story, "Following the Trail of Jesus." A number of years ago I felt as if I wanted to do something out of the ordinary to call attention to the subject of Divine Healing. So I went to the newspapers and posted $500. Then I announced that if anyone who was sick or diseased would come to the Healing Rooms and be ministered to for thirty days, and if at the end of that time they were not substantially better or healed, they could have the $500.

Over at Monroe, Washington, was a man by the name of Paul Gering, who had got to fooling around with spiritualism. That dear fellow was an open, splendid man. He was a hard working businessman. After he got to fooling with spiritualism, nobody could live with him. He was more like a raging lion than a human. He went all over the United States seeking deliverance from all kinds of folks who were praying for the sick.

He read my announcement and became interested. He sent me a telegram asking me to come to Monroe and put on a meeting, and of course, pray for him. He met Mrs. Lake and me at our hotel and drove us out to his home on the outskirts of the city. He walked into his home and stopped in the middle of the dining room and fell on his knees saying, "Mr. Lake, I am waiting for you to pray for me that I may be delivered." We laid hands on him and prayed and bless God, the power began to go through him. He was completely delivered, the demons were cast out, and he was baptized in the Spirit. From that time on hundreds of people have been saved and healed and baptized in the Holy Ghost under his ministry. Now he is a great wheat

Fire of God

farmer in the Big Bend country. Last night I spent the evening at his home and conducted a public service for his relatives and neighbors.

Just let me follow the trail of Jesus with you in that family for a few minutes. His sons were unsaved, his daughters were unsaved. One by one, after the father's deliverance, the faith of God in his heart laid hold on God for his family. They became converted and baptized in the Spirit until his entire family, including his beloved wife, was saved and baptized in the Holy Ghost.

Mr. Gering had a brother, Joe, a hard fellow and a heavy drinker. He owned a farm down in the country. His wife was distressed, for she saw he was gradually losing his grip on his affairs and squandering his money, and they were getting into financial difficulty. She was a woman of prayer and was praying for him. Finally one day he came to visit Paul Gering. Paul said, "Joe I am going to Spokane to attend Mr. Lake's meetings, come and go with me."

We were conducting meetings in our tabernacle. When they came, we were in the prayer room. The meeting went through without anything unusual occurring, until we were practically ready to dismiss. This man, Joe Gering, was sitting on one of the back seats. A lady turned to me and asked, "Who is that man on the back seat?"

I said, "That is Paul Gering's brother." She said, "the Lord told me to go and lay hands on him and pray, and he would be saved, and baptized in the Holy Ghost." I said, "Then you better go and do it sister."

She went back to him and engaged him in conversation and finally asked if she might pray with him. He said he had no objection to her praying for him. So she laid her hands on him and began to pray and as she did, the Spirit of God from heaven came down on him, and in a few minutes he yielded his heart to the Lord and prayed through until he got a real witness from

-288-

heaven and began to rejoice in the Lord. After he rejoiced for a while she said, "Now you ought to be baptized in the Holy Ghost." He knelt down again and began to pray, and after a few minutes Joe Gering was baptized in the Holy Ghost. That man's soul was so full of rejoicing that he spent the entire night singing and praying and rejoicing and talking in tongues and sometimes in English. In a few days he was out among the sinful and sick and getting folks saved and healed.

Here is another portion of the story. These men had a sister who lived at Palouse, Washington. She was unfortunately married to a very wicked man. She developed a tumor, and he insisted on her being operated on. She tried to tell him that in their family the Lord always healed them. He would not listen and insisted she be operated on. They brought her to St. Luke's Hospital in Spokane and she was operated on. A dreadful infection developed and they wired to the family that she was going to die, so the family began to gather here to see her. I knew nothing of these circumstances.

I was riding up Monroe Street when the Spirit of the Lord said, "Go to St. Luke's Hospital and pray for Paul Gering's sister. She is dying." I went immediately and inquired at the office and was directed to her bedside. I laid my hands on her and began to pray, and the Spirit of the Lord came upon the woman, the infection was destroyed, and in ten minutes she was sound asleep and the next day was on the highway to a blessed recovery. These are some of the things that take place when folks get into the line of God.

Their old mother was a godly woman who lived at Palouse. She had been notified that her daughter was likely to die, and when she got the word she went into her closet and interceded with God and prayed for the daughter's deliverance. I believe before God that when God spoke to me it was the answer to that mother's prayer. He sent help through me, and the Lord made her whole.

Fire of God

Gerber Girl's Healing

One day Mrs. Lake and I were present in a gathering of Christian people where these Gering people were and some of their neighbors. A family by the name of Gerber had a girl 17 or 18 years old. She stood up with her back to us, and I remarked to Mrs. Lake, "Did you ever see such a perfect form? That girl would do for an artist's model." But when she turned around I was shocked at her appearance; I never saw anyone so cross-eyed. It was a dreadful sight.

Later I talked to the father and he told me that surgeons would not undertake to straighten her eyes. They said it was impossible, and if they undertook it she was likely to lose her eyesight. Presently the young girl came over our way and I said, "Sit down, little woman, I want to talk to you." After talking a few minutes I stood up and laid my hands on her eyes. The Spirit of God came upon her and in three minutes' time those eyes were as straight as they were supposed to be. She is now married and has a beautiful home and lovely babies. Her eyes and heart are straight.

"Christ is at once the sinless descent of God into man, and the sinless ascent of man into God, and the Holy Spirit is the agent by which this is accomplished."

>Tongues and interpretation
>Somerset East Cape Colony, South Africa, June 1910
>
>Dr. John G. Lake

Obituaries

Fire of God

This book concludes with the obituaries of this man of God. He was used by God miraculously during his time on earth. He made himself available to the high calling of Christ and he remained faithful. God's anointing rested heavily on his life.

His life ended while he was pastoring in Spokane, Washington. His legacy continues even to this day throughout the world.

John G. Lake in Spokane

The Spokane Daily Chronicle   Monday September 16, 1935

DR. J.G. LAKE TAKEN BY DEATH

Dr. John G. Lake, pastor of the Apostolic tabernacle, Sharp and Lincoln, died early this morning at the family home. He suffered a stroke on Labor Day and failed to rally. Last week it was reported from the home that he was showing some improvement.

He was well known in Spokane and on the Coast as a healer and it is said that he had cured many afflicted with illnesses who had been given up by physicians. He had conducted religious work in Spokane on several occasions, the last time coming here from Portland four years ago. Some years ago he secured a frame tabernacle building on Sharp, where he has been in charge. He had spent 10 years in Spokane altogether.

Born in Canada

The Rev. Mr. Lake was 65 and is survived by his widow, Florence M.; five daughters, Mrs. Edna Ferguson of Lewiston, Mrs. Irene Robinson of Pendleton, and Gertrude, Elizabeth and Esther, all at the home; seven sons, Alexander and Otto B. of San Francisco; Horace and John G. Jr. of Portland; Wallace S. of North Bonneville, Wash; Livingstone G. and Roderick S. at the home; a brother, Wilford, in South Africa, and a sister, Mrs. Bertie Scott of Michigan. The body is at Hazen and Jaeger's.

The minister was born in St. Mary's Ont., Canada, and was educated in Michigan. He was a missionary in South Africa for six years and returned to the United States in 1912, remaining in the east until 1914, when he came west. Dr. Lake was a former Methodist minister and at one time was associated with the Rev. Alexander Dowie.

Fire of God

The Spokesman Review			Tuesday September 17, 1935

DR. LAKE DIES AFTER STROKE

Clergyman won Wide Interest in Connection with Divine Healing

The Rev. Dr. John G. Lake, spectacular figure in the religious world and leading exponent of divine healing died early yesterday at this home, W. 1523 Indiana. His illness started with a stroke on Labor Day.

Dr. Lake came to Spokane in September 1914, and established his own church of which he was a pastor for six years. For 11 years he worked with churches he had established in Portland, in California and in Texas. One year he was engaged in newspaper work in Oakland, dropping out of the ministry because he had lost his voice. Four years ago Dr. Lake returned to Spokane and had established his church in the large frame tabernacle on Sharp and Lincoln.

Funeral services will be held at 2:30 Wednesday at Hazen & Jaeger's, to be conducted by Evangelist, Irene Poupore, who has been conducting special meetings at the Lake Tabernacle. Burial will be in Riverside Park.

Was Disciple of Dowie

Dr. Lake was a disciple of John Alexander Dowie, who was at the height of his glory in Chicago. Dowie had become almost a national figure through his preaching of the doctrine of divine healing and people flocked to his Chicago tabernacle

John G. Lake in Spokane

from all over the country. It was Dowie who founded Zion City, near Chicago.

Dr. Lake went to Johannesburg, South Africa, in 1908, just after the Boer war, as one of Dowie's missionary group. He was in Africa five years, and in that country buried his first wife, who was the mother of seven children, all of whom returned to this country; two daughters, Mrs. Ferguson of Lewiston and Mrs. Clark Robinson; and three sons in Portland and two in San Francisco. The second wife and five children survive. They are Livingston and Gertrude, who have finished high school; Roderick, Elizabeth and Esther.

Joined Forces With McInturff

At one time Dr. Lake joined forces with Bishop D.N. McInturff, holding services in the old Vincent Methodist church at Main and Lincoln. They failed to agree and the congregation was divided, each having a following. The caretaker happened to be a friend of Bishop McInturff and carried the keys. The effect of the division was that the Lake faction was locked out and had to establish itself elsewhere. Both men were pronouced exponents of divine healing.

Fire of God

The Spokesman Review   Thursday September 19, 1935

MOURNERS WEEP AT HEALER'S RITES -CROWDS ATTEND-
Evangelist's address is interrupted often by "Hallelujahs,"

Nearly 700 people filled the Hazen & Jaeger undertaking establishment to overflowing yesterday afternoon for the funeral services of the Rev. Dr. John G. Lake, founder and Bishop of the Apostolic Lake Faith Church. The Alwin Chapel where the body lay ranked by flowers was filled long before the service was to begin.

The doors were thrown open to a second chapel and it quickly filled. Chairs were placed in the halls and in the reception room. They soon were taken and many stood. The loud speakers were turned on and the service was heard in all parts of the building.

MANY WALK WITH CANES

Old people both men and women were in the majority. Tears poured down their faces as the three clergymen spoke of the marvelous faith cures of Dr. Lake in Spokane. Many young people were present, even small children. Several middle-aged people were there on crutches and many walked unsteadily with canes.

Many brought beautiful flowers from their own gardens which attendants laid about the casket or placed in vases and containers around the walls. Virtually all the flowers, it was said were grown in the gardens of Dr. Lake's followers.

John G. Lake in Spokane

RICH AND POOR THERE

In the audience were newsboys and clergymen, rich and poor. In the 21 years Dr. Lake had carried on his ministry in Spokane, they had remained loyal to him worshipping in many different buildings and finally in the Lake Tabernacle just a block away from the scene of the funeral.

His favorite songs were sung by a trio consisting of Miss Esther Erickson, Miss Lillian Stone and M. E. Moser. They sang "Oh thou in Whose Presence," "At Calvary" and "Crown Him." Dr. Lake's favorite passages of Scripture were read by the Rev. Fred Wilson and Rev. R. S. Hebden.
"AMENS" are Frequent

Both clergymen spoke ardently of their association with Dr. Lake telling how he had found them years ago in poor health and had been instrumental in restoring their health and reviving their faith. During their talks there were frequent interruptions of "Amen," "God be praised" and "Hallelujah." They praised Dr. Lake's life and as a kind and loving father, a devoted husband and an inspired spiritual leader.

The Rev. Irene M. Poupore, evangelist at the Lake Tabernacle delivered the eulogy, she declared she was the first convert Dr. Lake had in Spokane years ago and said she had never had another minister who exalted the faith as did Dr. Lake.

When he came to Spokane, he found us in sin, sick, in poverty and in the grip of despair. She said, "We had thought victory was up there, but Dr. Lake taught us it was here."

SPEAKERS SHOW EMOTION

The evangelist was almost overcome with emotion during her address and had difficulty in continuing. She paid a tribute to the first Mrs. Lake who died in South Africa and to the present Mrs. Lake. "Our Mrs. Lake" as she called her. All seven children by the first marriage and the five by the second marriage, all 12 children are still alive.

The speakers variously referred to Dr. Lake as "brother" and "father" and "Doctor." His Apostolic Faith Mission, they said, had been started by him in South Africa. Returning to Spokane in 1914 he launched it here and ultimately opened other churches in Portland and San Diego.

Burial was in Riverside Park.

The Man We Are Proud Of

REV. JOHN G. LAKE
OUR PASTOR
The Most Remarkable God Anointed Preacher in the City

John G. Lake in Spokane

The Spokane Press   Thursday September 19, 1935

HUNDREDS GO TO DR. LAKE RITES

In the flower-filled Alwin Chapel of the Hazen and Jaeger funeral home final services for the Rev. John G. Lake were conducted Wednesday afternoon. His followers, young and old, were there in great numbers, filling the chapel and all adjoining rooms.

Dr. Lake founded his Apostolic Faith church in Spokane in 1914 upon returning from his mission in South Africa. Later he established churches in Portland and San Diego. The Rev. Irene M. Poupore delivered the funeral address, praising Dr. Lake as an evangelist and faith healer.

Flowers heaped about the chapel were said nearly all to have been grown in the gardens of his devoted followers.

The Rev. B.S. Hebden read passages of scriptures, Miss Esther Erickson, Miss Lillian Stone and M.E. Mosier sang Dr. Lake's favorite hymns.

The Apostolic Tabernacle in which Dr. Lake preached is situated at W. 824 Sharp. Internment was in the Riverside Park Cemetery.

Fire of God

The Spokane Daily Chronicle   Thursday September 19, 1935

WIDOW SUCCEEEDS SPOKANE HEALER

Mrs. Florence M. Lake, widow of the late Dr. John G. Lake, pastor of the Apostolic tabernacle, will be in charge of the work in Spokane, it was announced today by Mrs. Lake.

The Rev. Mrs. Irene Poupore, evangelist, who has been conducting services in the tabernacle, and an early convert of the Rev. Mr. Lake, will be pastor until a permanent pastor is named.

The Rev. J.S. McConnell, interdenominational evangelist; formerly of New York City, and now with headquarters in Seattle, begins a revival campaign at 7:45 tonight in the tabernacle, Sharp and Lincoln. He will be assisted by his two children, Grace, a vocal soloist, and John Jr., song leader. Meetings will be held for several weeks with services each night, except Saturday, and at 3 and 7:45 p.m. Sundays. Tonight's theme will be "God Coming Down."

Here once before

The evangelist was here about 12 years ago and conducted special meetings in a tent. In 1922; while conducting a revival in Walla Walla, he was forced from the pulpit by 60 men, he said and was taken into Oregon. However, he was allowed to return without harm and continued his meetings.

The Apostolic work here will have the assistance of other church leaders, including the Rev. Roy Whitfield, who will continue outside work among the sick. He has been an assistant of the Rev. Mr. Lake.

Funeral Services for the Rev. Mr.Lake held Wednesday afternoon in Hazen and Jaeger's chapel were attended by more than 600. All the chapels, side rooms and other parts of the

John G. Lake in Spokane

funeral home were occupied. The services were conducted by the Rev. Fred Wilson, in charge of the Apostolic work in Portland, evangelist Poupore, and B.S. Hebden. Internment was in Riverside Park.

Many attended the last rites from various communities in the Inland Empire and also from Portland.

Fire of God

Bibliography and personal study reference

Fire of God is the newly revised edition of the Anointing Fall on Me: John G. Lake 10 book series originally published in the Pacific Northwest Region of the United States in 1990. This is the first time since that limited release that the interviews the author conducted with Dr. Lake's parishioners have been released for a larger audience with permission.

Sermons included were taken from the Spokane newspapers.

Articles from the three Spokane newspapers have been used and citations included for each.

Addresses for Dr. Lake and his contemporaries during their time in Spokane:

Rev. John G. Lake -	West 1523 Indiana (1935)
Rev. Charles Westwood -	East 418 Liberty
Rev. Frank J. Osborne -	West 1115 1st
Rev. David N. McInturff -	North 28 Madison
	West 629 Nora (1933)
Rev. Chas. R. Hollandsworth -	2434 Wiscomb (1933)
	East 1108 11th (1936-)
Rev. Bernard S. Hebden -	West 3224 Gordon Ave. (1932)
	South 413 McClellan (1943)

Burial Place

Rev. John G. Lake - Riverside Memorial Park, Spokane, WA
Charles Westwood - Riverside Memorial Park, Spokane, WA

John G. Lake in Spokane

For more information about the Riley Media Group LLC, please access our website at Rileybooks.com or write to

Riley Media Group LLC
PO Box 8127
Spokane, WA 99203-0127
U.S.A.

Rileybooks.com